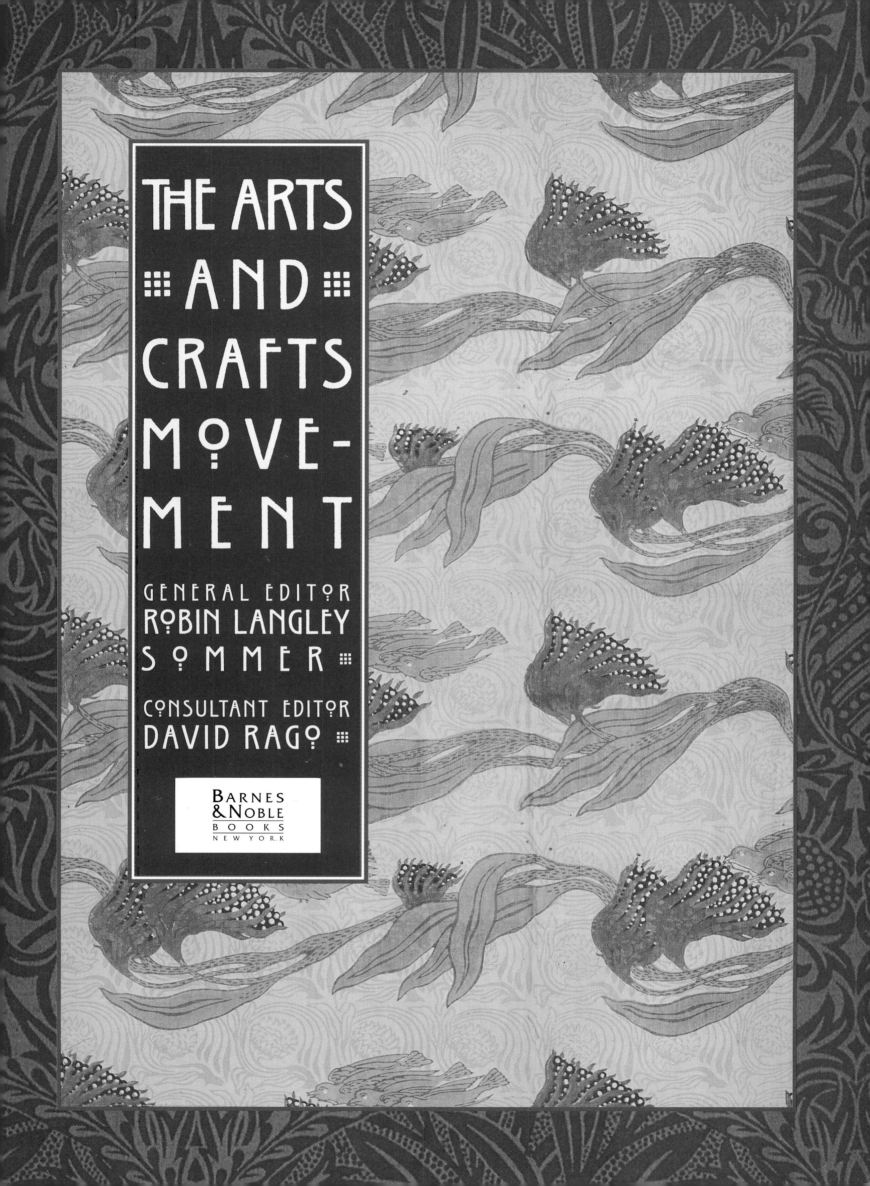

THE ARTS ▦ AND ▦ CRAFTS MOVE- MENT

GENERAL EDITOR
ROBIN LANGLEY
SOMMER ▦

CONSULTANT EDITOR
DAVID RAGO ▦

BARNES
&NOBLE
BOOKS
NEW YORK

This edition published by Barnes and Noble, Inc., by arrangement with Saraband (Scotland) Limited, The Arthouse, 752-756 Argyle Street, Glasgow G3 8UJ, Scotland.

2003 Barnes & Noble Books
Copyright © 2003 Saraband (Scotland) Ltd.

First edition © 1995, Saraband
Design © Ziga Design

Library of Congress Cataloging in Publication Data available

ISBN: 0-7607-4222-7

Printed in China

10 9 8 7 6 5 4 3 2

THE CONTRIBUTORS

MARIA COSTANTINO is a lecturer in art history and has written numerous books on design and the decorative arts, as well as a monograph on Frank Lloyd Wright. She grew up in Chicago, and has taught in the United States as well as in England, where she has lived for over ten years.

PATRICIA MORRIS graduated in Art History of Africa and South East Asia at the school of Oriental and African Studies in London, and in European Art History at University College, London where she specialized in art and design of the modern period. She is a keen collector of ceramics and tribal art and lives in Cornwall, England with her young son.

DEAN SIX is a collector and student of art glass, an interest which has been in his family for several generations. He is co-author of a book on American Cameo Glass and edits a collectors' newsletter on the subject; he writes for two popular glass periodicals, has contributed to a book on Seneca Glass Co., and has participated in an award-winning documentary about the glass industry. He has been an officer in numerous glass societies, co-founded the West Virginia Museum of American Glass in 1992, and established an annual regional glass history conference. He is currently working on an encyclopedia of glass production in his home state of West Virginia.

CONTENTS ⠿

INTRODUCTION

"ONE MAN'S THOUGHTS CAN NEVER BE EXPRESSED BY ANOTHER: AND THE DIFFERENCE BETWEEN THE SPIRIT OF TOUCH OF THE MAN WHO IS INVENTING, AND OF THE MAN WHO IS OBEYING DIRECTIONS, IS OFTEN ALL THE DIFFERENCE BETWEEN A GREAT AND A COMMON WORK OF ART."

— JOHN RUSKIN, 1853

The Arts and Crafts Movement represents a crucial period in the history of the decorative and applied arts, whose influence was to permeate the entire spectrum of design and craft work in Europe and America, helping to elevate crafts and the applied arts to a new status as valid art forms. Towards the end of the twentieth century, a hundred years after the peak of the movement, Arts and Crafts design is enjoying a strong resurgence in popularity. Yet the movement's origins were rooted as deeply in social ideals as they were in aesthetic principles; the British founders did not, in fact, strive to create an identifiable visual "style." Rather, for them, it was a philosophy, even a way of life, involving society and its relationship to art as much as art itself. They had a vision of quality of life through design, craftsmanship, the production process, and the environment.

Victorian Britain was a society experiencing increasing industrialization and population growth, with expanding cities and a new middle class. Working conditions in factories were harsh, sometimes dangerous, and urban low-income housing standards were dismally poor. The Socialist movement was beginning to raise awareness of inequality and the need for social change, giving rise to middle-class philanthropic sentiments.

Attitudes to, and changes in, design—from the blighted urban environment to industrial goods—reflected these developments. There was a growing reaction to the "anti-design" trend of industry and mass production, part of a more general resentment of the tyranny of the machine. Rebellion against the dominance of machines was voiced by philosopher Thomas Carlyle, who wrote in an 1829 essay: "Nothing is now done directly by hand; all is by rule and calculated contrivance…the living artisan is driven from his workshop." The Great Exhibition of 1851, while a success on its own terms, highlighted the decline in British design standards. Ever-growing demand for housing, together with new technology in the form of iron and steel framing, as well as concrete, led to a need for new perspectives in architecture.

A. W. N. Pugin (1812–52), an architect and critic who was strongly inspired by medieval influences, had introduced the tenet that architecture's value depended on "the fitness of the design to the purpose for which it was intended" (*Contrasts*, 1836). Since early Victorian times, there had been a gradual revival of interest in Gothic architecture in Britain, as opposed to the prevailing styles, particularly neo-Classical, which dominated the period. Pugin argued that the rigid demands of Classical form in building precluded serious consideration of the function of the building in its design; by contrast, medieval builders had created their own working designs, mindful of the use of the building, and without the artificial constraints of symmetry or particular external shapes or styles imposed by a separate designer.

These two themes of the utilitarian value of Gothic architecture, and the de-emphasis on design in machine-dominated industry, were expanded upon by John Ruskin, the leading art and architecture critic of mid-nineteenth century Britain and the major formative influence in the Arts and Crafts Movement. His major works influencing design principles were *The Seven Lamps of Architecture* (1849), *The Stones of Venice* (1853) and *The Two Paths* (1858–9). Rejecting the methods of Victorian industry, Ruskin stated that medieval standards of care and craftsmanship gave rise to the beauty of the buildings and the ornamentation of the period. Such beauty and quality, he believed, could be achieved *only* by the skilled hand labor of artisans, and not by machines, irrespective of the design. Not only quality, but also individuality and creativity, were sacrificed in commercial machine production. In his essay "The Nature of Gothic," Ruskin emphasised that medieval designer-craftsmen had freedom of expression, creating buildings and interiors whose style followed no prescribed form. The needs of the buildings' intended users dictated the structure, while the ornamentation and interiors were designed in a sympathetic style by

the same craftsmen. The result was a unified whole: a utilitarian structure furnished and decorated from one aesthetic vision, unfettered by preconceived stylistic rules.

Strongly influenced by Ruskin's writings, William Morris became the true founder of the Arts and Crafts Movement. Morris (1834–96) broadly agreed with Ruskin's aesthetic theories, and combined them with his Socialist beliefs — prompted by his revulsion against Victorian society—to formulate his complex opinions on art, design, and society. Machines, for Morris, could be *beneficial* to society when employed in tedious,

Above*: William Morris, founder of the Arts and Crafts Movement, wearing an artist's smock, from a photo taken for a visiting card c. 1870. Morris was tireless in his efforts to elevate the decorative arts to fine-art stature.*

Below: Kelmscott Manor, the 16th-century country house Morris leased in Oxfordshire to provide a broader base for his experiments in the decorative arts. He furnished the house with Eastern ceramics and furniture of his own design, combined with English traditional.

repetitive tasks degrading to a manual laborer. But, in addition to producing an inferior result, as Ruskin had pointed out, he also believed they were dehumanizing—in replacing the work of artisans, they undermined the dignity of skilled labor. In Gothic architecture, he, too, appreciated the utilitarian approach, the freedom of expression, and the quality of workmanship. Not only did he wish to restore these values, he wanted to transform Victorian working conditions to allow the worker a more satisfying involvement in all aspects of a project, as in medieval times. In this, he echoed the Marxist analysis of capitalism's division of labor. His ambitious goal was to bring together the roles of designer and craftsman, to make hand-crafted quality products commercial and widely available,

and to improve working and living conditions at the same time.

Morris began his career in 1856, as an apprentice to the architect G.E. Street. There he met senior draughtsman Philip Webb (1831–1915), who shared Morris's attitudes. In 1859 Webb designed for Morris the first Arts & Crafts building, the Red House, in Kent, England. Home to Morris and his bride Jane Burden (a Pre-Raphaelite model), it was functional and unpretentious, beautifully furnished and decorated by Morris and his friends and colleagues, including Edward Burne-Jones, the Pre-Raphaelite painter (a college friend), and Dante Gabriel Rossetti, the artist and poet. The building stood apart from contemporary architecture: it was asymmetrical, and its unusually shaped exterior was not elaborately ornamented.

Shortly afterward, in 1861, the firm of Morris, Marshall, Faulkner and Co. was launched: "Fine Art Workmen in Painting, Carving, Furniture and the Metals," aiming to "produce harmony between the various parts of a successful work" (quotation from their first prospectus). The firm, reorganized in 1875 as Morris and Co., produced furniture, metalwork, stained glass, carvings, tiles, textiles, murals, and wallpaper, designed and made by artist friends as well as the members, often employing motifs of flora and fauna. These motifs, particularly as seen in the firm's rugs, tapestries, and graphic art, reflected a respect for nature, as well as the growing influence of Japanese painting on mid- to late-nineteenth century European art. Morris went on to open the Kelmscott Press in 1890, developing distinctive typography and elaborate book designs, as well as manufacturing books.

An increasingly difficult problem for Morris was the contradiction between his democratic ideals and the expense inherent in his hand-crafted, high-quality products. His "objects of beauty" were, inevitably, beyond the reach of all but the privileged and well-off, who received the firm's goods with enthusiasm. Morris could resolve this contradiction to some degree through advocating (and practicing) good working conditions, not only by ensuring that his colleagues and craftworkers were able to derive satisfaction from their work, but also in following up some of the social ideals of philanthropic industrialists Robert Owen and Titus Salt. (These men had created self-sufficient schemes providing good housing, leisure facilities, and an attractive environment for their workers at New

Lanark, Scotland, and Saltaire, Yorkshire). For Morris, a lifestyle of "honest" work in pleasant surroundings was all-important, and participation in the making of good products was as important as owning them. Nevertheless, he remained uncomfortable that the fruits of the craftsmen's labors were enjoyed only by the "idle rich."

His reverence for the architecture of the Middle Ages led Morris to take a keen interest in the preservation of the Gothic buildings and artifacts he admired. In 1877 he founded the Society for the Preservation of Ancient Buildings, and he was actively involved in attempts to preserve the countryside, at a time when industry and urban growth were unhampered by regulation; indeed, preservation was a new concept. The abundance of rural land, wildlife, natural resources, and "old buildings" was still taken entirely for granted, despite the serious environmental problems associated with industrialization. Other members of the society included architects

Above: *A painted metal casket of Medieval inspiration executed by Morris for Kelmscott House. It shows the aesthetic of revealed construction, whereby rivets, banding, and various kinds of hardware are integral to the design. The warm, rich colors of the painted panels have the feeling of tapestry work.*

Below: Morris "Dove and Rose" fabric, c.1879. This fabric of woven silk and wool was produced at Morris and Company's Hammersmith, London, facility. It illustrates the rhythmic natural forms that figure so prominently in Morris's designs, and those of other early Arts and Crafts designers.

Webb, Ernest Gimson (1864–1920), and William Lethaby (1857–1931). Lethaby became one of the most influential figures in the Arts and Crafts Movement, his idealistic views of social reform and design closely aligned with those of Morris. The National Trust, founded in 1894, was dedicated to conservation. Among its founders was Canon Rawnsley, who set up the Keswick School of Industrial Art, an evening school for poor residents of this Lake District town,

which produced some excellent Arts and Crafts metalwork, and Octavia Hill, who worked to provide quality, well-designed low-income housing. Most luminaries in the British conservation movement took on, like these two, much of Morris's philosophy, while in turn, respect for the environment and working in harmony with nature became central preoccupations in the movement, both in and beyond Britain.

The ideas of Morris and his colleagues soon gained widespread influence. In 1882, architect Arthur Mackmurdo (1851–1942), in conjunction with other artists and craftsmen, established the interdisciplinary Century Guild, which was based on the medieval guilds or associations of craftsmen. They produced textiles, furniture, metalwork, and enameled goods, and founded the journal *The Hobby Horse*. A group of architectural assistants, including William Lethaby and Ernest Gimson, followed suit with the Art Workers' Guild, set up in 1884. The Guild of Handicraft, founded in 1888 by Charles Robert Ashbee (1863–1942), pursued goals similar to those of the Century and Arts Workers' Guilds, and added a more explicitly philanthropic element by recruiting local workers in the poor East End of London. With Ashbee's emphasis on the Guild's social principles, this profit-sharing, communal living experiment became an ideal in its embodiment of Arts and Crafts principles, thriving for over two decades.

These three Guilds, while London-based, had a national impact. The Birmingham Guild, created in 1890, produced important metalwork and jewelry, as well as another magazine, *The Quest*. The Birmingham School of Art, the Vittoria

Street School for Jewelers and Silver-smiths, and the Ruskin Pottery followed in the area. Similar craft schools and guild-style associations began to flourish throughout the country, sometimes with marked regional variations in styles and materials, as they incorporated elements of the local heritage.

The Glasgow School of Art ran a lecture series on the Arts and Crafts Movement in 1893, initiating a prolific period of artistic endeavor that developed into the Glasgow Style. Architect and artist Charles Rennie Mackintosh (1868–1928) was the most prominent figure, designing not only buildings but every conceivable detail of their furnishing, down to the cutlery. A fine example of his "complete" approach was the exquisitely appointed Willow Tea Rooms (1903). More geometric and abstract than the English styles, these distinctive textiles, furniture, metalwork, glass, and jewelry met with critical acclaim in Scotland, where the designs remain as popular as ever, and worldwide. It was especially influential in Vienna and contributed directly to the early development of Art Nouveau in France, also anticipating many of the themes of Frank Lloyd Wright's Prairie style in the United States.

As early as the 1880s, the movement had become a complex web of idealistic and stylistic elements. The initial emphasis on medievalism began to wane; neither the Glasgow school, nor such designers as Voysey, demonstrated its influence except in embracing utilitari-

Above: These two reverse-painted Handel table lamps, finely decorated with nature scenes, exemplify several of the common themes in the Arts and Crafts movement. Tree trunks and branches are worked on the bronze base of the right-hand lamp. Both have simple lines and soft, natural colors, designed and hand-crafted to the highest standards.

anism. The common threads that emerged in the movement's philosophical and social principles were: social reform of working conditions; free individual expression encouraging creative satisfaction and dignity in labor; regionalism and the use of local and natural, rather than imported or overly processed, materials; and the holistic unity of a building's design, furnishings, and adornments in harmony with its environment, respecting particularly the natural environment. A variety of styles and visual motifs were incorporated, both curvilinear, as seen in Morris's floral and other nature-inspired motifs and the Japanese influence, and rectilinear or geometrical. Despite the diversity, though, Arts and Crafts design was visually identifiable by its guiding principles of functionalism, simplicity, and lack of pretentious ornamentation, as well as the appearance of hand-crafted quality from fine, "honest" materials. Internationally,

the Arts and Crafts Movement was to develop in different directions from these origins, with each regional or national style taking on a mixture of some, but not all, of its characteristics.

In the United States, early Arts and Crafts activity began in the 1870s with an increase in the production of handicrafts, particularly among women. At the University of Cincinnati's School of Design, Englishman Benn Pitman had started classes in woodcarving and china painting, which were attended mainly by upper middle-class women. Among the students were Mary Louise McLaughlin, who became an accomplished furniture maker and potter, experimenting with ceramics glazes using both French and Japanese techniques; and Maria Longworth Nichols, who founded Rookwood Pottery in 1880. Using motifs from nature in painted china, and a variety of innovative as well as traditional glazing techniques (some of which were devel-

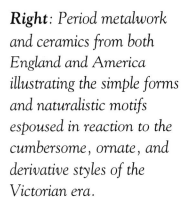

Right: Period metalwork and ceramics from both England and America illustrating the simple forms and naturalistic motifs espoused in reaction to the cumbersome, ornate, and derivative styles of the Victorian era.

oped from McLaughlin's), Rookwood's fine-art pottery products were a commercial success, and the company quickly became well known. Meanwhile, in New York, Candace Wheeler (1827–1923) had founded the Society of Decorative Arts in 1877; it provided crafts instruction modeled on London's Kensington School.

Women of many ethnic and economic backgrounds had always been involved in craft activity in America, whether to provide practically for the home, or, for more affluent women, as a hobby or accomplishment. The rise of such institutions as the Society of Decorative Arts gave talented women with a leisure interest in craft work the opportunity to refine their skills, learn new techniques, exchange ideas, and turn their crafts into paid, professional work. Wheeler herself specialized in needlework and embroidery, but she was interested in all the decorative arts. She operated a decorating business with L.C. Tiffany (1848–1933) for a number of years, before he set up independently as an art glass specialist, eventually becoming the nation's most influential and admired decorative artist.

As American society, like Victorian Britain, experienced growing urbanization and industrialization, with the added factor of large-scale immigration, public taste changed to reflect the times. Mass production could provide cheaper goods for the home, and domestic goods tended away from reproductions of ornate European styles toward simpler lines, particularly for the growing middle classes. Traditional home crafts and folk art of many communities became fashionable, from Shaker to Native American. Against a background of increased interest in

hand-crafted goods, and a preference for greater simplicity and economy in design, the Arts and Crafts Movement took off rapidly in late 1880s America. Where the British craftsmen had been inspired and led by intellectuals, and their products enjoyed mainly by an elite, the new American design reflected grass-roots involvement in crafts as much as abstract principles.

Chicago-based architect Frank Lloyd Wright (1867–1959) was one of the movement's most prominent figures. He began his career as an engineer's assistant before being apprenticed to Louis Sullivan, the highly respected Chicago School architect. Wright had no formal training in architecture and was guided by what he saw and imagined, rather than by the conventional wisdom. Ele-

Above: French-born American artist Elizabeth E. Burton designed this copper table lamp with shades of abalone shell, which filtered the light to a soft, muted glow. Electrical light fixtures provided a unique vehicle for combining the effects of color, iridescence, and patination.

Above: *American architect Frank Lloyd Wright, whose incredible body of work through a career that spanned 70 years would make him the single most important influence on 20th-century design.*

ments of both Japanese and pre-Columbian art, his two major stylistic interests, were manifest in his work—although he denied the direct influence of any visual style, claiming to have no preconceptions but to begin with the purpose of each building he designed.

Wright's architecture was innovative from his earliest days with Sullivan, whom he joined in 1887. He began

immediately to develop what became known as the Prairie style: functional buildings, often U- or T-shaped rather than the traditional "box" design; they were low-ceilinged with broad eaves and, sometimes, gabled roofs. Windows were relatively large and numerous, "to bring the outside inside," and interior partition walls were sometimes replaced with three-quarter-height screens to create a more spacious, airy feel. The Prairie style incorporated many variations, but Wright typically employed geometric lines (with a horizontal emphasis rather than Sullivan's vertical look), and built-in furniture and features such as tiled fireplaces or integrated window seats. Finishing was in natural shades like green and brown. Prairie houses were distinct from British Arts and Crafts architecture, although there were obvious similarities with Mackintosh and themes common to other architects in the movement: simpler, functional designs, the use of both local and natural materials, and the careful complementing of building and setting.

Elsewhere in Chicago, Jane Addams and Ellen Gates Starr founded Hull House in 1889—a settlement house in a poor neighborhood, where craft instruction was offered to the residents. Philanthropic social reform and charitable work were, like home-produced crafts, traditionally the province of women in nineteenth-century America. The work of voluntary women's groups in encouraging craft production, while campaigning for better low-income housing and other causes, paralleled some of the British Arts and Crafts institutions. In 1897 the Chicago Society of Arts and Crafts was established at Hull House, with Wright as a founding member.

Left: *The dinner service designed by Frank Lloyd Wright for the Cabaret dining room in Tokyo's grand Imperial Hotel (1916–22). Wright was responsible for every aspect of the project, from the infrastructure to napery and tableware. More than 700 drawings were involved.*

Morris-inspired craft-working communities were established in America, although they were less integral to the development of design than they had been in Britain. The Roycroft Press was set up in 1895 in East Aurora, New York, by Elbert Hubbard, who had visited Europe and wanted to emulate the printing and design of the Kelmscott Press, although he did not subscribe to Morris's social or political views. The venture was a success, first producing books and the journal *The Philistine*; then a bindery, leather work, furniture, glass, and metalwork production were added to the printing facility. Hubbard's background was in business rather than design, and the Roycroft community—some 400 work-

Below: *A period settle showing the clean lines and respectful craftsmanship that characterized the movement.*

ers — was a commercial enterprise in which Hubbard maintained control himself, paying his workers relatively low wages. However, conditions for the residents were very good in terms of working hours, variety of tasks and craftwork experience, and leisure and educational facilities, including libraries and lecture series. The Roycrofters enjoyed a lifestyle essentially in tune with the ideals of Morris and Ruskin, despite the substantial political and philosophical differences.

Two other New York-based Arts and Crafts communities were Rose Valley (1901–09), with over 100 workers organized communally in a rural setting modeled on the ideals of Ashbee; and the

Byrdcliffe Colony (1902–15) in Woodstock, founded by Ralph Radcliffe Whitehead, who had been a friend of Ruskin's. While these communities most closely resembled the British Arts and Crafts Movement and embraced social ideals as much as design, they were fairly short-lived, and neither achieved much financial success.

The simple, economical, handcrafted look of the products of early American Arts and Crafts institutions were in tune with the changes in contemporary popular taste. The mass production of emergent Arts and Crafts-style furniture would make it widely available, rather than the province of an elite who could afford handmade goods. The Phoenix Furniture Company and Charles Limbert Company, both in Grand Rapids, made furniture that reflected the Mackintosh style. These companies, and others, produced their furniture at affordable prices, often using veneers or cheaper materials as well as mass production techniques.

In Fayetteville, New York, near Syracuse, the brothers Leopold and J. George Stickley established their furniture company in 1902. They imitated the designs of their better-known brother Gustav Stickley (1858–1942), whose Craftsman furniture plant, founded in Syracuse in 1898, made him the leading figure in the American Arts and Crafts Movement. Dedicated to "honest art," Stickley had been profoundly impressed by Ashbee and others he had met in Europe, influences also obvious in the work of his architect colleague and most talented designer, Harvey Ellis. Stickley's Mission-style furniture was made of solid local oak rather than imported woods, beautifully and laboriously finished and stained with-

Below: *Gustav Stickley hutch with Dirk van Erp metal vase and art pottery from the Van Briggle and Grueby Faience companies, and tall case clock by L. & J. G. Stickley.*

out chemicals. The pieces were plain and functional, ornamented only by carefully crafted joints and the natural finish that enhanced the beauty of the wood.

The name "Mission" derived both from the influence of Spanish colonial church design and Stickley's credo that furniture must "fill its mission of usefulness as well as it possibly can." While the style was particularly associated with Stickley, who applied his "honest" principles to metalwork and other crafts as well as furniture, the Roycrofters and others produced Mission furniture that was widely imitated. Popular magazines like the Philadelphia-based *Ladies Home Journal* (whose editor, Edward Bok, lived in a home designed by Rose Valley architect William Price) regularly featured Mission furniture and Arts and Crafts architecture and interiors. Stickley himself published a highly influential design magazine, *The Craftsman*. It printed essays from Ruskin

and Morris, in addition to architectural sketches of low-cost bungalows — which he called "Craftsman Homes."

In Massachusetts, silversmithing, pottery, and fine book printing were among the most successful endeavors of the many new crafts organizations established during the 1890s. The Boston Arts and Crafts Society, established in 1897, embraced some of the movement's social principles and became a forum for local and national design ideas. More concentrated in the Boston area than anywhere outside Ohio, pottery flourished. The non-profit Paul Revere Pottery, founded in 1906, combined the movement's social and aesthetic principles. It was established in connection with the Saturday Evening Girls' Club, a social organization for immigrant families in the Boston area.

By the turn of the century, the Arts and Crafts Movement was well established in the Midwest and the Northeast, while

Above: *Grueby was best known for its distinctive green matte-glazed ceramics and tiles with plant motifs. Gustav Stickley helped to popularize the firm's wares through ads and illustrations in his magazine* The Craftsman.

Right: A warm, richly furnished interior from the David B. Gamble house (1908), designed and furnished by the Pasadena, California, architects Charles Sumner Greene and Henry Mather Greene. Wood was the Greenes' favorite medium, as seen in the sinuous lines of the joinery below ceiling level and at lower right. The fireplace surround is of architectural ceramic tile, and the living room is encircled by a redwood frieze carved in the Japanese ramma manner with mountains, trees, and vegetation from the surrounding landscape.

small studios had emerged in the South, including George Ohr's pottery in Biloxi, Mississippi, and Newcomb's of New Orleans. In the West, cities were booming in the wake of the Gold Rush and the new transcontinental railroad lines. Architectural fashions were mixed, from Victorian and Colonial to modern, experimental styles. In 1894 San Francisco's Golden Gate Park gained redwood pavilions and Franciscan Mission details, in the style of the previous year's World's Columbian Exhibition in Chicago.

The disastrous San Francisco earthquake and fire of 1906 created an urgent demand for reconstruction, drawing many new architects, builders, and furniture manufacturers to California. English architect Ernest Coxhead, and California's first woman architect, Julia Morgan, developed simple modern dwellings that sprang up widely during the reconstruction of the city. In southern California, Charles and Henry Greene, originally of Cincinnati, designed the homes and interiors that made Pasadena an architectural mecca by 1910. Their work drew inspiration from sources including low-gabled Alpine chalets and articulated Japanese structures and landscaping.

Others who carried Eastern and Midwestern Arts and Crafts design influences to the West were writer, teacher, and tilemaker Ernest Batchelder and furniture designer Louis B. Easton, Elbert Hubbard's brother-in-law. In the Pacific Northwest, Bay Area and Prairie-school influences were apparent, as seen in the Alaska-Yukon Exposition of 1909. On a smaller scale, pioneers like Colorado's Artus and Anne van Briggle worked in home craft studios. Few vestiges of the Gothic or Queen Anne Revival styles remained in the Western Arts and Crafts Movement by the early 1900s. The new regional look was the result of Spanish Mission, Native American, and Prairie-school elements, with design simplicity and emphasis on indoor-outdoor living.

While the Arts and Crafts Movement developed in the United States, its influence was also spreading through Europe. Again, many designers did not share the social ideals of Morris and his colleagues, nor their distrust of industrialization and machine production: those countries that had never fully industrialized had no reason, in fact, to reject it. But there was profound European interest in the design ideals of the British movement. *The Studio* magazine was widely subscribed to abroad, and many European designers visited Britain to view the exhibitions of the various societies and guilds. The craft ethic—the honest use of materials, good design for objects in everyday use, and the ideal of design unity—was recognized and praised.

Below: *Flower boat with handle designed by Dutch-born coppersmith Dirk van Erp, who established his influential Arts and Crafts studio in San Francisco in 1910. The Dirk van Erp studios produced a variety of art metalware, including copper lamps that figure in many period interiors.*

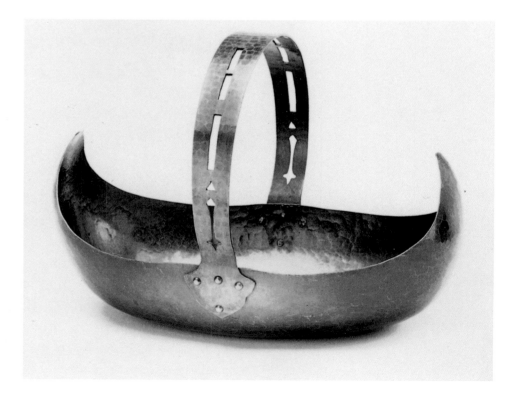

Right: The mark of Vienna's Wiener Werkstätte, an arbiter of Continental design co-founded by Josef Hoffmann in 1902. Strongly influenced by the aesthetic of British designers Ashbee and Mackintosh, the Wiener Werkstätte *produced hand-crafted metalwork, furniture, textiles, leather, graphic designs, and complete interiors.*

Throughout Europe, as in Britain and the United States, the search for national self-expression was manifested in a growing interest in conservation, national history, legends, and folkways. Numerous guilds and associations based on British models sprang up. Many Scandinavian associations focused on reviving traditional craft techniques and styles, like the *Handarbetets Vänner* (Friends of Textile Art Association, established in Sweden as early as 1814); the *Suomen Käsityön Ystävät* (Friends of Finnish Handicrafts), founded in 1870; and the *Föreningen Svensk Hemslöjd* (Swedish Handicraft Society), set up in 1899.

Home industry associations emerged in Transylvania (now part of Romania), and the region became a center for the study of vernacular design. Hungary's *Gödöllő* artists colony, founded in 1903 and led by Aladar Korosfoi-Kriesch (1863–1920), was a Utopian community based on the belief that a return to handicrafts could have a transforming power in people's lives. Through reviving such crafts, the colony gave the rural poor a reason for staying on their lands rather than emigrating to the cities or to the United States.

In France and Belgium, the Arts and Crafts Movement strongly influenced, and was soon virtually supplanted by, the emergent architecture and decorative arts styles of Art Nouveau. There were, however, some innovative craftsmen who were both widely known and emulated by Arts and Crafts designers in the United States and Europe, such as French art potters Théodore Deck, Ernest Chaplet, and Auguste Delaherche.

Impressed by the writings of Ruskin and Morris, Austrian Josef Hoffmann (1870–1956) visited Ashbee's Guild of Handicraft in 1902 and returned to Vienna to establish a similar organisation: the *Wiener Werkstätte*. Many of the designers had been trained at the *Kunstgewebeschule* (School of Applied Arts), where the designs of C. R. Mackintosh and Baillie Scott were much admired. The *Werkstätte* produced hand-crafted metalwork, furniture, textiles and leather, and distinctive graphic design. Although the *Werkstätte* used machinery, as well as licenced manufacturers working from its designs, its products remained expensive: Hoffmann refused to compromise his high ideals of craftsmanship and good design.

Most of the workshops established in Germany toward the turn of the century focused on machine production rather than hand-crafting. The first and most influential of these, the *Vereinigte Werkstätte fur Kunst im Handwerk* (United Workshops for Art in Craftsmanship), was founded in Munich in 1897 by Richard Riemerschmid (1868–1957). On the whole the German associations shared the belief that design should be objective and rational, based on efficiency and functionalism.

Craftsmen like Hoffmann, who doubted that art and industry could ever be united, saw this as an attack on individuality and creativity. These opposing views were eventually brought together in Germany in the *Deutsche Werkbund*, founded in 1907 by Riemerschmid, Hoffmann, Josef Olbrich and others. It included artists, designers and manufacturers united in the pursuit of good design. Despite ongoing dissension between opposing factions within the *Werkbund*, its exhibitions and publications were influential in promoting German design and cooperation between art and industry. Peter Behrens (1868–1940), spent several years designing for craft production before his appointment as artistic advisor to the electronic firm *Allgemeine Elektricitäts-Gesellschaft* (AEG) in Berlin. There he adapted his Arts and Crafts background to a more industrial approach, designing electrical appliances, factory buildings, workers' housing, and a unified company identity based on his graphic designs. The stylistic legacy of these German institutions and the wider Arts and Crafts Movement was the Bauhaus Movement, begun by Walter Gropius in 1919.

From the nature-inspired handcrafted goods of Morris and his colleagues, through the honest, unadorned pieces of Gustav Stickley, and the functional lines of Frank Lloyd Wright, this book illustrates a richly varied selection of the Arts and Crafts Movement's architecture, interiors, furniture, glass, metalwork, ceramics, textiles, and graphic art, fashioned by those who were dedicated to the highest standards in design. The authors have described the major developments in, and influences on, each craft or medium, the leading figures and institu-

tions, and their techniques, styles and philosophies, as well as selecting a diverse and representative range of subjects for the plates. Each chapter features the work of the leading craftsmen and designers in their fields, as well as that of less well-known artists who shared their ideals and made a contribution to the movement. The book combines the considerable expertise of each contributor, and of the consultant —Arts and Crafts historian, collector, and photographer David Rago — to provide both an informative overview and a beautiful photographic album of a movement that continues to increase in popularity.

Above: Josef Hoffmann's exuberant design for Vienna's Cabaret Fledermaus (1907). The cabaret is in striking contrast to the Workshop's first important commission, the austere, geometric Purkersdorf Sanatorium, designed by Hoffmann and Koloman Moser in 1904–5.

ARCHITECTURE, INTERIOR DESIGN

The first landmark of the Arts and Crafts Movement was built for William Morris at Bexley Heath in Kent by Philip Webb (1831–1915) in 1859. The Red House, the result of a new collaboration between architect and artist, was so called simply because it was built of red brick, at a time when stucco was fashionable. While there is an awareness of the past in its use of pointed arches and such interior details as the elongated newel posts of the staircase, the building was designed primarily as a functional, practical, and comfortable home. Departing from the classical facade, which conceals the interior layout, Webb allowed the function of interior spaces to dictate the whole design, and introduced a line of rooms along a corridor that formed an L-shape around the courtyard to give a sense of intimacy. The entrance hall is dominated by the first of Morris's huge built-in furniture pieces, a combination of hall cupboard and seat decorated with painted panels. Similar large built-in pieces also appear in the drawing room, including the famous white-painted settle cupboard topped with a miniature minstrels gallery. In the dining room is an enormous scarlet-stained and iron-hinged cupboard by Morris and Webb which proved too large to move!

Due in part to the growing popularity of Morris and Associates in the decorative arts, in part to Webb's rejection of architectural stylism, the Red House was to become a major influence on a new generation of architects, encouraging them to give pre-eminence to function and to select materials and forms appropriate to the local landscape and traditions.

Richard Norman Shaw (1831–1912) succeeded Webb as chief draughtsman in the Oxford-based architectural practice of G.E Street (1824–81), where

Right: Charles Limbert furniture with Grueby vase. Arts and Crafts furniture on both sides of the Atlantic was deeply indebted to the designs pioneered by William Morris, including the classic Morris chair. Sturdy simplified forms worked together to create the functional, comfortable home that was one of the movement's primary objectives.

AND FURNITURE

Morris himself had been an apprentice in 1856. There he learned a love of crafts and made a study of traditionally built houses in Yorkshire, Kent, and Sussex. For his larger houses, which were deliberately asymmetrical, Shaw combined half-timbered upper floors topped by tall, decorative chimneys with local stone or brick lower storeys. His smaller Queen Anne-style London townhouses (from the 1870s) combined elements of Dutch gabling, classical motifs, and brick. Webb and Shaw were the two major figures in the British domestic revival movement.

W.R Lethaby (1857–1931), former assistant to Shaw and a leading member of the Art Workers Guild, combined traditional building methods with such technical innovations as concrete. His Church of All Saints, Brockhampton, has a concrete roof capped with thatch, a traditional Herefordshire roofing material. Design freedom meant that both form and materials could be used in new, experimental ways while allowing for individual interpretations of Arts and Crafts principles.

The principle of design unity in the Arts and Crafts Movement applied not only to Arts and Crafts buildings themselves, but to their ambient landscapes, gardens, and interior furnishings. The leading Arts and Crafts garden designer in Britain, Gertrude Jekyll (1843–1932), was a follower of Morris and a self-taught silversmith and embroiderer. Garden design favored indigenous British flowers—a fashion inspired in part by Morris's use of native plant motifs in his textile and wallpaper designs. In partnership with architect Edwin Lutyens, Jekyll expressed Morris's ideas on design unity in over 100 British gardens, including those masterworks at Sonning, in Berkshire, and Hestercombe, in Somerset.

While some Arts and Crafts architects bought furnishings for their clients from the new class of professional antique dealers, others, like Baillie-Scott, Mackintosh, and Voysey, saw their buildings as wholly integrated projects. In his furniture designs, Baillie-Scott took Morris's dictum of having only beautiful objects in a house one stage further: for him, beauty was contingent upon appropriate use and position as well as craftsmanship. The placement of each interior design component, whether an oaken door or an elmwood table, was crucial. Baillie-Scott developed a number of features characteristic of Arts and Crafts interiors: the hearth, with deep ingles, served as the heart of the home, and the infrequently used "dead" space of entrance halls was transformed into the "dwelling-hall," reminiscent of medieval

Left: The texture of textiles, including carpets and embroidered cushions and hangings, enriched the look of hand-finished wood furniture, metalwork lamps and sconces, and simple vases of stone- and earthenware, all elements working together to form a harmonious setting.

Below: *The simple elegance of this Charles Limbert cabinet makes it an exemplar of movement furniture design, whose major exponents included Morris, Harvey Ellis, C. R. Mackintosh, and America's Gustav Stickley and the Roycroft craftsmen. Oak was a primary material in both Britain and the United States, but more exotic woods like mahogany and redwood were used by California Arts and Crafts designers.*

architecture in its use of half-timbering and painted wall panels.

Both Baillie-Scott and the Glasgow architect C.R Mackintosh used fitted and moveable furniture in their quest for decorative unity. They also devised "color codes" to differentiate between traditional men's and women's rooms: white walls and furniture were used in bedrooms, drawing rooms, kitchens and bathrooms (the traditional women's domains) while dark oak furniture dominated the more "masculine" spaces like billiard and smoking rooms. Mackintosh was to take the principle of the integrated interior further by designing as many details as possible for his clients, including decorative friezes, light fixtures, carpets, silverware, and even cutlery. Comfort was essential for Arts and Crafts designers, including C.F.A Voysey (1857–1941), whose passion for craftsmanship was matched by a concern for economy. He believed that houses should be light, easy to clean, and inexpensive to run. Whitewashed walls, large tiled fireplaces, white or natural-oak beamed ceilings, and hard-wearing slate floors figure in many of his commissions, including The Homestead, Frinton-on-Sea, and his own house, The Orchard, at Chorleywood.

The "garden cities" of the early 1900s realised some of the ideals espoused by Ruskin and Morris in response to the dehumanization inherent in the Industrial Revolution. Morris advocated communities based on the model of 14th-century rural village settlements, while Ruskin saw the solution in the careful planning of new cities. The roots of the garden city movement had been struck earlier in the century by a handful of philanthropic industrialists in the north of Britain: Robert Owen's New Lanark was established in central Scotland in the 1810s to house and educate workers in his cotton mills. Sir Titus Salt's model estate, Saltaire, was set up near Bradford in 1850, and William Hesketh Lever's Port Sunlight was built on Merseyside in 1889. The term "garden city" was coined by Ebenezer Howard (1850–1928), who was influenced not only by Ruskin but by the American transcendentalist Ralph Waldo Emerson and the poet Walt Whitman. Howard insisted that each planned town or city, like an Arts and Crafts building, should relate to its chosen site and be guided by economic research that tied it to other communities. In 1903 Howard helped to found the Garden City Pioneer

Company and a plan for the first city—Letchworth, in Hertfordshire—was submitted by Lethaby and Ricardo. However, this plan was defeated in the design competition by that of Unwin and Parker, who had previous experience in planning the estate of New Earswick, in Yorkshire, for chocolate baron Joseph Rowntree. Letchworth New Town was successful in attracting professional men and women dedicated to a simpler and more fulfilling life. They were often ridiculed by the popular press, but a government report published forty years later stated that the citizens of Letchworth were healthier by far than the inhabitants of any other industrial town.

The idea that each nation should have an architecture that reflected its history, climate, and geography was central to the Arts and Crafts Movement, whose call for a revival of vernacular architecture was enthusiastically answered all over Europe and in the United States. There, interpretations of the vernacular varied widely, in keeping with the nation's ethnic diversity. On the West Coast, architects and designers looked to the Spanish missions for inspiration; in the Midwest it was the wide expanses of the prairies, with their pioneer heritage. On the East Coast, with its close ties to the British Colonial past, architects adapted such styles as the Gothic, Tudor, and Queen Anne Revival.

The Gothic style was especially favored for church architecture: Bertram Grosvenor Goodhue (1869–1928) and Ralph Adams Cram (1863–1942) designed a number of influential houses of worship, ranging in size from the small-scale St. John's Church in West Hartford, Connecticut, to the imposing St. Thomas

Church in New York City. Cram and Goodhue were among the founders of the Boston Society of Arts and Crafts, modelled on the English Arts and Crafts Exhibition Society which held its first exhibition in 1898. Boston's status as a cultural center helped spread craft ideals nationwide via the society's salesrooms and exhibitions and encouraged the growth of similar groups.

During the 1870s and 1880s, New England architects began fusing elements of the Queen Anne style—red brickwork, sunflower motifs, and broken pedi-

Above: The Ladies' Home Journal *for March 1899 awarded this Wellesley, Massachusetts, house in the Queen Anne Revival style high honors in its contest for "The Prettiest Country Homes in America." The interior drawing above it is captioned "Design for a Dining-Room, Giving Rustic Effect."*

Below: A California Mission-style house with characteristic adobe-type walls (often stucco on frame construction), red tile roof, and simple rectilinear lines varied by arched entryways inside and out. A patio was usually concealed within a courtyard formed by adjoining walls, while the street side of the house was simply planted and unadorned. The Spanish Colonial Revival style found acceptance far beyond the Southwest, especially in other warm climates like that of Florida.

ments—with the half-timbering of Tudor-style buildings. H.H. Richardson (1838–86) adopted the half-timbering that Norman Shaw had restored to English use, but he replaced hung tiles with shingles—a roof and wall covering widely used during the colonial period. A Dutch Colonial revival style became popular in the mid-Atlantic states like New Jersey and Delaware, which had been colonized by the Netherlands during the seventeenth century. This style, popularized by Aymar Embury II (1880–1966), was characterized by broad roofs and large chimneys and fireplaces, with stone walls for the lower storeys and shingled exteriors for the upper floors.

In California Charles Sumner Greene (1868–1957) and his brother, Henry Mather Greene (1870–1954), were the outstanding exponents of Arts and Crafts architecture. On one of his many visits to the United States, C.R. Ashbee admired the brothers' work and compared it favorably with that of Frank

Lloyd Wright, with whom Ashbee had become friendly in the late 1800s. While Wright championed the use of machine technology, the Greenes favored hand craftsmanship, though all three agreed on the importance of high-quality materials. The Greenes had become aware of crafts at Calvin Milton Woodward's Manual Training High School in St. Louis and went on to study at the Massachusetts Institute of Technology. A major influence on their later work was Gustav Stickley (1858–1942), the gifted furniture designer and architect who did so much to bring English Arts and Crafts ideals to the American public. Stickley's Craftsman Workshops in central New York State produced furniture appropriate to the livable low-cost bungalows and comfortable two-storey houses he designed. From 1901 Stickley published the influential magazine *The Craftsman*, which included plans and specifications for his houses. Clients could also have the designs built for them by Stickley's company.

Another important influence on the Greenes was Oriental art: like Wright, they collected Japanese prints and books about Oriental gardens, furniture, and architecture. All these influences converged in the Greene brothers' "ultimate bungalows," designed between 1907 and 1909. The low verandahed bungalow style, originated in the Far East, was ideally suited to the Southwestern climate. Native redwood was used for construction and mahogany for the furniture, demonstrating the versatility of beautiful wood in the hands of craftsmen. The Gamble house (1908–09), with its protruding rafters and elaborate bracket supports, offered protection from the Cali-

fornia sun and ample space for outdoor living in the form of porches and terraces. Exterior and setting were in harmony, unified by the Greenes' landscaping and their designs for furniture, rugs, lighting fixtures, and stained glass with recurring geometric motifs.

While most Californians could not afford a Greene & Greene custom-designed house, they could still conform to Arts and Crafts ideals by living in either a wood-frame bungalow or an adobe (mud brick) mission-style house. Alfred Heinemann (1882–1974) designed and built several hundred attractive bungalows in Pasadena; plans were available for a mere $5.00, and the cost of construction was about $3,000. Architect John Gill (1870–1936) had trained with Frank Lloyd Wright's mentor Louis Sullivan (1856–1924) in Chicago for two years before moving to San Diego in 1893 for health reasons. In the regional mission architecture, Gill saw perfect geometric forms combined with plain undecorated surfaces inside and out. Gill used this vernacular form to design the low-cost, hygienic housing that was his primary concern.

The most innovative American regional style was that of the Prairie School, originating in the Midwest with the architecture of Frank Lloyd Wright (1867–1959). Influenced by Sullivan's ideas on an "organic architecture," Wright evolved the design language that brought this concept to life in such dwellings as the Frederick C. Robie House (Chicago, 1906). It exemplified Wright's use of large, free-flowing living areas, well lighted by windows that opened the house to continuous views of the grounds, making the setting integral

to the design. Fireplaces, screens, and other design elements served to distinguish the various living areas without the rigid demarcations of the traditional "box" house. As far as possible, Wright persuaded his clients to furnish their residential and commercial buildings with furniture, stained glass, lighting fixtures, textiles, and accessories of his own design.

For those who could not afford architect-designed furniture, help was at hand from designers and manufacturers like Charles Rohlfs (1853–1936); Arthur and Lucia Kleinhans, founders of the Furniture Shop in San Francisco; Gustav Stickley's Craftsman Workshops at Syracuse, New York (or his brothers' companies in Fayetteville, New York, and Grand Rapids, Michigan); the Shop of the Crafters in Cincinnati; or the Roycroft Shops in East Aurora, New York, founded by Elbert Hubbard (1856–1915), where furniture was first sold to the public in 1897. At Roycroft, hand-hammered copper products and simple rectilinear furniture influenced by A. H. Mackmurdo were produced until 1938. The Roycrofters' furniture, of unvarnished native wood with minimal ornamentation, adhered closely to Arts and Crafts ideals. The movement's high standards could encompass objects made in almost any medium: simple "honest" materials and pride in the way they were fashioned to serve their purpose in the home or workplace were the hallmarks of Arts and Crafts design.

Above: Advertisements for moderately-priced houses abounded in turn-of-the-century magazines like The Ladies Home Journal *and* Gustav Stickley's Craftsman *magazine. The* mail-order catalogue of Sears, Roebuck and Company offered pre-cut components and blueprints for houses that its customers built all over the country.

THE RED HOUSE, KENT, PHILIP WEBB (above)

The house that Webb designed for William Morris and his bride, Jane Burden, in 1859 had a far-reaching effect on period architecture. Warm and unpretentious, medieval in its inspiration, it was described by Dante Gabriel Rossetti as "more a poem than a house." Richly but comfortably furnished by Morris and his talented friends, it presented an intimate alternative to the dramatic medieval designs of London's William Burges (1827–81).

STANDEN, EAST GRINSTEAD, SUSSEX (opposite, above)

This distinguished country house, seen from the garden, was designed by Webb in 1891 and built of native stone, brick, tile, and weather-boarding. Its unusual features include recessed sash windows in panels and tall chimneys at right angles to one another. Standen reflects the axioms added by Webb and Richard Norman Shaw to British architecture: freedom of expression in terms of design and materials and an increased awareness of local tradition.

WILLIAM MORRIS BED, KELMSCOTT MANOR, 1862 (opposite)

This massive four-poster bed was designed by Morris with mottoes on the top panel—an innovation that was widely adopted by movement designers—and printed hangings in his early style.

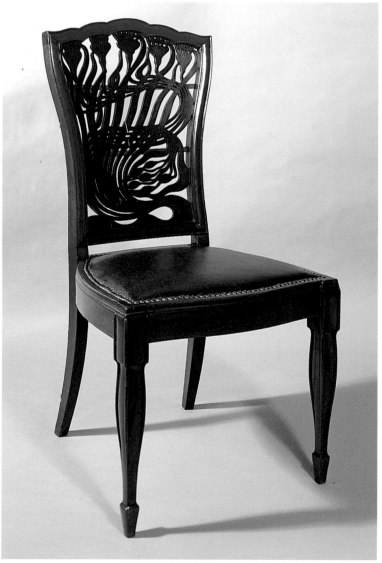

PHILIP WEBB FURNITURE GROUP, 1860S *(above)*
Rush-seated ebonized armchair, settle, and side chair similar to seating designed for the Red House by Dante Gabriel Rossetti and marketed by Morris & Company as the Sussex line.

A. H. MACKMURDO DINING CHAIR, C.1882 *(left)*
Designed for the Century Guild, this dining chair with fretwork back is an impressive example of Mackmurdo's work, which reflects his training as an architect. His mentor James Brook was an architect-craftsman whom he described as designing "every detail to door hinge and prayerbook marker."

MORRIS & COMPANY RECLINING CHAIR, C. 1865 *(opposite)*
One of many variations on the so-called Morris chair, this reclining armchair designed by Philip Webb is upholstered in the "Daffodil" chintz fabric. This and the distinctive woodwork give it an opulent Oriental quality.

C. R. MACKINTOSH PERSPECTIVE DRAWING, 1901 (left)

This perspective drawing for Glasgow's Daily Record buildings was executed in pencil, ink, and watercolor. The challenge posed by a poorly lit site was overcome by providing a generous number of windows and using reflective white glazed brick above the street-level masonry. The skyline dormers and corbelled cornice derive from Scottish vernacular architecture.

MACKINTOSH CLOCK, 1905 (above)

This clock formed of a cube supported by 16 square columns was designed for Walter Blackie, Hill House, in 1905. The design was replicated by Mackintosh for his own home, where it is now displayed in the reconstruction of his drawing room. A similar clock was made in 1917 for client W. J. Bassett-Lowke's house at 78 Derngate, Northampton.

MACKINTOSH HOUSE DINING ROOM, 1906 *(above)*

The University of Glasgow's Hunterian Art Gallery has reconstructed the principal rooms, including the dining room, from the Mackintosh House at 78 Southpark Avenue, Glasgow, the home of Mackintosh and Margaret Macdonald Mackintosh from 1906 to 1914. The original terraced house had been significantly remodelled by Mackintosh six years after his marriage and furnished throughout in his distinctive style.

HVITTRÄSK, LAKE VITTRÄSK, FINLAND 1901–03 (above)

Eliel Saarinen, often called Finland's national architect, designed this home-studio with his partners Herman Gesellius and Armas Lindgren. Built on a lakeside ridge west of Helsinki, the building rises dramatically from its granite foundation, linked to the site by stone walls, terraces, pavilions, and porches. Local building materials include granite, plaster, and logs, with pantiles and shingles for the roofs. Hvitträsk is actually a series of structures, one free-standing and the others connected with skylighted studios, in the manner of Frank Lloyd Wright's Taliesin East and West, in Wisconsin and Arizona.

HVITTRÄSK, LIVING ROOM (opposite)

The deeply arched ceiling, doorways and generous hearth in the Finnish vernacular give this interior the sense of shelter so valued by period architects. It embodies the Arts and Crafts ideal of design unity, known on the Continent by the German word Gesamtkunstwerk—a total work of art. Traditional brick and metalwork, textiles in the style of the Friends of Finnish Handicrafts, fireplace frieze and furniture, much of it designed by Saarinen, have made the house a national symbol comparable to the Finnish Pavilion designed by the same group for the 1900 Paris Exposition Universelle.

GUSTAV STICKLEY FURNITURE GROUP, C. 1900 *(above)*

A spindled cube settee with higher cornerposts is flanked by a clip-corner square table with lower shelf surmounted by an embroidered period textile and a copper lamp with conical shape and flaring base. The floor covering is a boldly patterned geometric rug.

DETAIL, G. STICKLEY DESK HARDWARE *(right)*

This hammered-copper handle was designed for a ladies' drop-front desk of metal and wood inlaid with stylized flowers produced by the Craftsman workshops around the turn of the century.

TALL STAND, ROYCROFT SHOPS, C. 1903 *(left)*

This simple, heavy stand of oak, the Roycrofters' major material, was designed to hold books, magazines, or objects for display. Maple leaves incised on each side comprise the only ornament apart from the tenons and joints. Roycroft furniture drew much of its inspiration from the prevailing Mission style and was commercially successful due to the marketing skills of founder Elbert Hubbard. After Hubbard and his wife died in the 1915 sinking of the Lusitania, Elbert's son Bert Hubbard directed the business. The community's best-known designer was Dard Hunter, who made furniture, metalwork, and books influenced, after 1908, by the Viennese Secession style. His successor was Karl Kipp, who directed the large metal workshop until 1912, producing hammered-copper vases, trays, lamps and other furnishings.

GUSTAV STICKLEY LIBRARY TABLE WITH LAMP, C. 1906 *(below)*

This hexagonal leather-topped library table was a popular design, usually made in quarter-sawn oak with metal studs. Gustav Stickley furniture designs were widely imitated and eagerly acquired by middle-class householders.

SHOP OF THE CRAFTERS ARMCHAIR & DINING CHAIRS (above)

These inlaid and upholstered pieces with slatted backs have a more luxurious look than most period designs from the major American furniture makers, including those of Gustav Stickley's brothers: the L. and J. G. Stickley Company of Fayetteville, New York, and Stickley Brothers in Grand Rapids, Michigan, the major furniture center in 1900. The shop of the Crafters was based in Cincinnati, Ohio.

HARVEY ELLIS DROP-FRONT DESK, 1903 (left)

This graceful ladies' drop-front desk with inlaid design is typical of the work of Harvey Ellis, who began his career as a draughtsman in Albany, New York, during the early 1870s. There he collaborated with architect H. H. Richardson on designs for the state capitol building. He went to work for Gustav Stickley in 1903, already well known for his sensitive graphic artwork, and was featured prominently in the Craftsman magazine until his untimely death the following year.

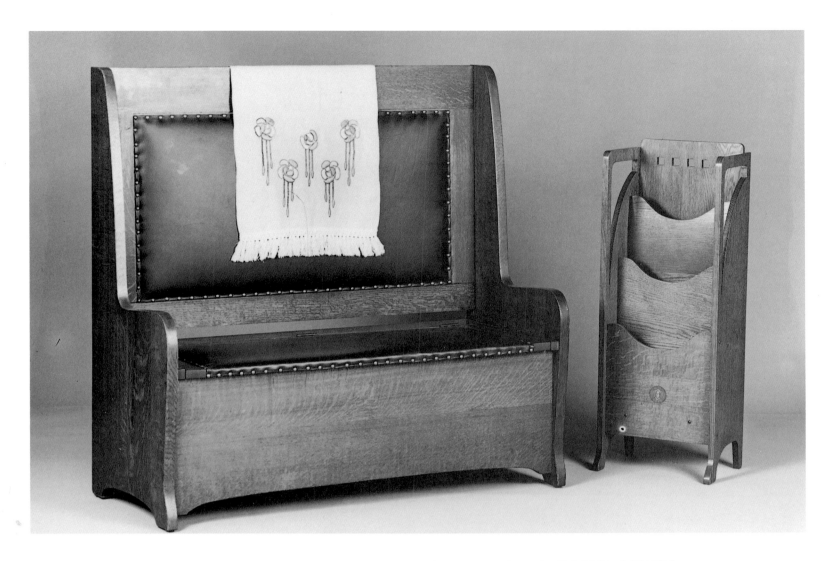

PERIOD SETTLE, MAGAZINE RACK, & TEXTILE (above)

Oak seating with leather upholstery and complementary pieces in the same wood figured prominently in furniture catalogues of the early 1900s. A heavy "permanent" settle like this was often used in an entryway, in contrast to the movable settle with slatted back and sides, which could be shifted readily from room to room. Both types might be upholstered with soft cushions rather than leather. Embroidered runners fringed at both ends were commonly used to cover bureaus and tabletops.

PEWABIC POTTERY, DETROIT, MICHIGAN *(above)*

This Arts and Crafts-style building, with its half-timbered facade and panels of upstairs windows, was used by Mary Chase Perry as a factory for her porcelain and ceramic artwares from 1903. She produced vases of simple form fired in the Revelation kiln invented by Horace J. Caulkins and decorated with rich iridescent glazes. Her career as a potter extended into her nineties.

FRANK LLOYD WRIGHT DINING CHAIR *(opposite, left)*

Wright's austere high-backed dining chairs, seen opposite in the Meyer May house at Grand Rapids, Michigan (1908), were designed to create the feeling of a room within a room around the dining table. The sense of enclosure was enhanced by the built-in lighting fixtures on piers at the corners of the table. Wright experimented with the design at his Oak Park, Illinois, home-studio in the late 1880s and used it for many Prairie House interiors. The only drawback, several clients protested, was that the chairs were uncomfortable.

DINING ROOM, MEYER MAY HOUSE, 1908 *(above)*

This interior from Michigan's Prairie House masterpiece is dominated by vertical elements, including the high-backed chairs and the four corner piers that support the dining table. They are surmounted by lights that translate the planes of the art-glass windows into three-dimensional boxes with angled tops repeating the carpet motif. Every feature was designed by Wright except for the glowing mural at top left, the work of artist George Niedecken.

FRANK LLOYD WRIGHT FRICKE HOUSE, 1901 (above)

Built for William G. Fricke of Oak Park, Illinois, this early Prairie House design is essentially vertical, even as Wright was moving toward horizontal dominance. The broad over-hanging eaves and dark horizontal banding of windows are balanced by the three-story central tower and the projecting bays of living room and reception room. The main entry leads to a central hall from which ground-level rooms fan out in a clockwise pattern. The stucco walls were treated like masonry, which makes the house a precursor of the mono-lithic Unity Temple (1904), also constructed in Oak Park.

WRIGHT'S STORER HOUSE, LOS ANGELES, 1923 (opposite)

The two-story living room of this textile-block design for John Storer has a sense of grandeur, derived from the tex-tured concrete pillars and the long sweep of the room to a terrace at either end. The house's southern exposure has a hilltop view of Hollywood and Los Angeles, while the north-ern view is into a courtyard carved from the hillside. Wright maintained a Los Angeles office from 1917, from which he supervised the construction of seven houses for southern California clients.

STORER HOUSE ENTRY HALL *(above)*

The imposing entry hall at ground level has a colonnade of textile blocks, influenced by pre-Columbian design, and a golden mural of wisteria by L. C. Tiffany. The heavy hanging light fixtures are in keeping with the scale, as is the massive urn on its low platform. Skylights prevented the entryway from feeling dark or oppressive as one entered from the expansive sunlit terrace flanked by plantings. Frank Lloyd Wright's son designed the landscaping.

BARNSDALL HOUSE ENTRY COURT & POOL *(opposite, above)*

Stylized hollyhocks in cast concrete, which Wright called art stone, surmount the entry to the house's garden court, flanked by a loggia. Miss Barnsdall's favorite flower gave the house its name and recurs as a decorative motif throughout the complex. The basic structural material is a clay tile, and the art stone ornaments were made from crushed decomposed granite at the site.

BARNSDALL (HOLLYHOCK) HOUSE, 1917 *(above)*

Actress and director Aline Barnsdall first met Frank Lloyd Wright in 1914, but designs for the house she called her "California Romanza" were delayed until she purchased the 36-acre Olive Hill site overlooking Los Angeles in 1919. The living room fireplace rises from a reflecting pool on the south wall, surmounted by an art-glass ceiling light trimmed with oak. The project was actually a complex of four buildings designed to serve as a gathering place for artists and friends of the client, which helps to explain its monumental character.

LA JOLLA WOMEN'S CLUB, CALIFORNIA *(opposite)*

This serene enclosure within a concrete structure of simple rounded rooms is typical of the work of California architect Irving Gill. He had trained with Dankmar Adler and Louis Sullivan in Chicago at the same time as Frank Lloyd Wright, and his style tended toward the removal of ornament. One of his major concerns was the construction of moderate-cost concrete housing, several examples of which exist in San Diego.

GAMBLE HOUSE, PASADENA, 1908 (above)

Architects Charles Sumner Greene and Henry Mather Greene designed this Japanese-influenced house, a culmination of the California Arts and Crafts style, for David B. Gamble. The front porch is an abstraction of a Japanese temple gate, which both shelters the inhabitants and frames the landscape. The house radiates out on several different levels, with terraces and gardens to bring the outdoors inside. The shingle-covered exterior rises naturally from the surroundings.

GAMBLE HOUSE LIVING ROOM (above)

The richness of this interior is due to the deep tones of redwood and mahogany, with sinuously carved wooden forms delineating the fireplace, set in California ceramic tile. The interior is not brightly lighted; rather it has a hushed, contemplative darkness relieved by the muted light from metalwork fixtures designed by the Greenes. In the front door, a great California oak is portrayed in Tiffany glass by Emile Lange. The Greenes not only designed the furniture and fixtures, but executed many of the carvings themselves.

DINING ROOM, GAMBLE HOUSE (left)

The flow of living space from one area to another is reminiscent of Frank Lloyd Wright's Prairie House style, but the Japanese influence is more apparent than in most of his designs. Rich Oriental carpets cover portions of the glowing wooden floors to help define the various living spaces. The Greene brothers designed several "bungalows" in this mode for wealthy clients in Pasadena, and their designs gained wider appreciation through publication in the Craftsman magazine.

▦ GLASS

lass design and production did not respond to the Arts and Crafts aesthetic as simply as did most other materials. The concerns raised by Ruskin, Morris, and others about industrial mass production did not as readily or neatly apply to the creation of glass.

The hand pressing of glass began in the 1830s, replacing centuries-old fully hand-crafted techniques. With the technological leap of hand pressing, it was possible for the first time to produce a volume of identical items quickly and economically. Nevertheless, mechanization and industrialization did not have as radical an impact on glass production as on other materials; well into the 1920s, the glass house remained a hand-craft facility, even with hand pressing.

A working definition of Arts and Crafts glass has yet to be written. As diverse regional styles developed within the Arts and Crafts Movement, glass products appear even more disparate in style than other media; only scant dividing lines separate them from Art Nouveau, Art Moderne, the Bauhaus, and other movements. The look of simplicity and minimal adornment, particularly apparent in American Arts and Crafts buildings and furniture, did not apply to Arts and Crafts glassware, in part because of the imaginative use of glass—particularly windows—as adornment and as part of the creative use of light. It is impossible to find common stylistic threads among Burne-Jones's stained glass windows, the 1890s proto-Art Nouveau creations, and the severe geometry of Frank Lloyd Wright. The unifying feature of Arts and Crafts glass is seen in its role in its creators' search for "quality of life," encompassing both process and end result. In the words of the *Wiener Werkstätte* manifesto, "usefulness is our first requirement and our strength has to lie in good proportions and materials well handled." In defining Arts and Crafts glass, the criteria must be material integrity, artistic control over the creative process, and a fusion of craft with fine art, rather than any visual motifs.

Before studying the body of work within this definition of Arts and Crafts glass, the processes need to be considered. As a material, glass is treated in two distinct ways: it can be used cold, as a fragile play with light in windows, architectural elements, lamps, and lighting fixtures. It can also be manipulated hot, as a fluid: liquid shaped into vases, bowls, and art objects of endless forms. Hot and cold glass

Right: Frank Lloyd Wright art glass, abstraction of the prairie sumac plant. Several variations of this design were installed in the Susan Lawrence Dana House at Springfield, Illinois (1903). The Linden Glass Co. of Chicago fabricated the windows to Wright's design.

played different roles within the Arts and Crafts movement. Pre-formed sheets of cold glass could be used in ways comparable with the use of wood in creating furniture. Frank Lloyd Wright, Hungary's *Gödöllō* colony, and others used glass panels in this way; cut into elaborate shapes and leaded, glass sheets were made into mosaic-like windows. In the creation of light fixtures, glass was cut and set in bronze or other metals, as in the work of Dard Hunter for the Roycroft Shops. A design could be conceived, sketched, considered, revised, and created by the artist, far from the industrial anonymity of a factory. By contrast, the use of hot glass in creating art objects involved completely different processes and techniques. Extending the wood-and-furniture analogy of cold-glass methods, the hot-glass process would equate to carving wood to form a sculpture instead of using pieces to construct an object.

Traditionally, glass is formed at the mouth of a furnace heated to 2,400° F (1,315° C) when it is in the form of a slow-moving liquid "glob." Within minutes of removal from the heat source, the glass solidifies and becomes rigid and brittle; it can no longer be worked. Thus, the creative process of forming a hot-glass piece must be completed quickly, drastically restricting the creator's ability to design and form objects. Hand-formed glass may have gradations of color applied by the addition of different-colored layers, or glass can be added to specific areas to create a design. This must be accomplished while manipulating an intensely hot molten mass. The significance of the brevity of the creative encounter cannot be underestimated. Before beginning, the artisan must have a clear vision of the intended shape, which must be translated skillfully into form quickly enough to avoid failure. Thus, it was virtually impossible for hot-glass production to conform to the Arts and Crafts ideal of designer-craftsmen working on a whole project in different media, since the experience and speed required for this medium were so highly specialized.

Hot- and cold-glass techniques, then, were employed within different facets of the movement. Cold-glass methods could be incorporated within the artist-colony

Below: Stained glass panel Minstrel *depicting an angel with cymbals, designed by William Morris and produced by William Morris & Co. c. 1880.*

Above: *Agate vase, blown and molded, c. 1897. Louis C. Tiffany design produced at the Tiffany Glass facility at Corona, Long Island, New York.*

via special paints. Thus, for example, the face of a character in a stained glass window is painted and the paint or "stain" is then fired at a much lower temperature than that of the melting point for glass to affix it. These individually stained pieces are joined by metal strips to form the window. Not all colored-glass windows are technically stained glass. Tiffany achieved color variances in windows by manipulating layers of varied hot-glass colors. Wright used cold glass of various colors and clear glass to create his visual palette. These windows are properly called leaded rather than stained glass.

The *Gödöllő* workshops (1902–1921), near Budapest, Hungary, incorporated Arts and Crafts ideals as a way of life. There, Aladar Korosfoi-Kriesch created an artists' colony that explored many forms, from weaving to graphic arts and glass windows. The influence of Hungarian folk art is seen in the work of Sandor Nagy, one of *Gödöllő's* best-known glass creators. In Nagy's hands, Transylvanian ballads became memorable stained glass windows.

In England, the window design work of Henry George Alexander Holiday (1839–1927) combines the idealized Pre-Raphaelite style with Arts and Crafts freedom and visual vocabulary. Trained at the Royal Academy Schools, Holiday worked as a stained glass cartoonist for Powell's of Whitefriars, for whom he designed many exceptional windows. Harvey Ellis, a Rochester, New York architect, also designed windows, furniture, and illustrations. Ellis became known when his works appeared in *The Craftsman*.

Flat glass was widely employed in the construction of lighting fixtures. The rise

approach of the Roycrofters and the guilds and the principles of holistic building design espoused by Frank Lloyd Wright or Mackintosh. The creation of art objects in hot glass was a skilled endeavor in which the craftsman was also the designer. Both types of process fused craft with fine art.

The basic technology for creating leaded and stained glass windows dates to Medieval Gothic cathedrals. The Arts and Crafts Movement made windows an integral part of architecture and design when employing stained or leaded glass, which are not synonymous. Stained glass involves cutting pieces of glass into elements of the design, then adding details of the Arts and Crafts movement coincided with the availability of electric lighting and gave birth to new opportunities. The Roycrofters of East Aurora, New York, made lighting fixtures and many other objects at their artists' colony, established by Elbert Hubbard on communal lines. Dard Hunter was a Roycroft designer; he made electric lamps of wood with glass panels, compatible with the Roycrofters' furniture designs. Hunter visited Europe and was much influenced by Viennese design.

While electric and other lighting fixtures are often considered metalwork in their use of copper, bronze, and other materials as bases and leading, they can equally be seen as primarily glass objects. They are made to filter, color, and control light, whatever its source, and their artistry consists in the interplay of glass and light. Crossover artists like Ernest Batchelder, a California ceramist, used glass panels successfully in executing cop-

per-and-glass electric porch "lanterns." Architects Charles Sumner Greene and Henry Mather Greene, who worked in Pasadena, used glass and metals for the lights in their innovative Gamble House. Arts and Crafts creators outside the glass realm found it technically possible to design for the inclusion of glass panels in objects made of mixed materials.

C.R. Mackintosh, the Glasgow architect and designer, allowed for the inclusion of sheet glass in lighting fixtures and his furniture often included leaded glass in doors and panels. His electric ceiling fixture for the Room-de-Luxe in the Willow Tea Rooms of Glasgow shows great playfulness in its use of suspended glass globes. This free-form use of glass strikes an entirely different visual chord than such work as his rose-themed leaded-glass screen panels for the Modern Decorative Arts Exhibition of 1902.

Glass vessels were equally diverse. One design approach was to enclose an

Left: *John La Farge altar window for St. Paul's Episcopal Church, Stockbridge, Massachusetts, in vibrant colors of green and ruby red. It depicts St. Paul preaching to the Athenians on Mars Hill.*

⠿ GLASS

Right: Leaded-glass sconce comprising a Gustav Stickley bracket of hammered copper and polished translucent glass panels of various colors in geometric shapes: circles, rectangles, diamonds, and octagons. This type of lighting fixture became extremely popular and was widely produced by Arts and Crafts glass designers.

unadorned bottle, vase, or pitcher in a metal mount. Here the "design" work could be executed in silver, copper, or some other material to enhance the glass without addressing the complications of hot-glass production. Silver designs by C.R. Ashbee were executed by the Guild of Handicraft, and Christopher Dresser mounted simple glass claret jugs in silver. The use of metalwork to encase glass was more usual in Great Britain than abroad. Other Dresser designs were blown in hot glass, influenced by Morris in their simple and organic shapes. "Clutha" glass— fluid shapes showing bubbles and the marks of hand crafting—was a Dresser design executed by James Cooper & Sons of Glasgow.

The windows created by *An Túr Gloine* (The Tower of Glass), founded in Ireland by Sarah Purser in 1903, were a cooperative effort. Its craftsmen included many women who worked together on designing, glass selection, and execution. *An Túr Gloine* was managed by A.E. Child, a teacher at the influential Dublin Metropolitan School of Art and a student of Christopher Whall, who has been called the father of English Arts and Crafts stained glass. The Dublin school conducted a stained glass workshop that did important work in the medium. Other significant Irish artisans include Wilhelmina Geddes, who created the Duke of Connaught War Memorial in Ottawa, Canada, and Harry Clark, a gifted illustrator who produced many Arts and Crafts windows.

In the United States, no stained or leaded glass windows are better known than those of Louis Comfort Tiffany. Initially, the guildlike Associated Artists executed his designs. In 1885 Tiffany founded his own Tiffany Glass Company, which produced windows, lamps, and other lighting fixtures from sheet glass, much of it manufactured at Tiffany's own glass furnace in Corona, New York. This was unusual in combining hot-glass production and window execution, which afforded greater artistic control. Like other creators, Tiffany blended the benefits of technology and hand crafting. While his leaded table lamps were made by hand, many of them carried a pattern number; thus identical designs could be executed in various colors.

The windows designed by Frank Lloyd Wright included such stylized motifs as the Tree of Life. Much of Wright's work was geometric, even stark, as compared to Tiffany's leaded glass windows. The Avery Coonley Playhouse windows show Wright's masterful use of light as a true design element. The leaded glass for the Martin House in Buffalo, New York, was executed, like many Wright commissions, by the Linden Glass Co. of Chicago.

Wright's clear-glass windows "brought the outside in" and set new standards for American architecture that were widely admired and emulated abroad.

Vienna's *Wiener Werkstätte* designed significant Arts and Crafts glass, but due to the special requirements of producing hot glass, the group never manufactured it. Production was executed by J & L Lobmeyer and E. Bakalowits Söhne. Designs were the work of Koloman Moser, Josef Hoffmann, and other artists engaged at the *Wiener Werkstätte*. By 1915 they began to acquire glass blanks to which decoration was applied. They utilized hand-painted and fired-on decorations, and, later, incised designs. Their hand-painted designs constitute some of their most recognizable work, representing different talents within the *Wiener Werkstätte*.

In the United States, L.C. Tiffany encouraged hot-glass employees to create and experiment, a freedom that contributed to the diversity and success of Tiffany's glass. Studio lines bore such names as "Favrile," which means "hand made," consistent with Arts and Crafts principles but with an entrepreneur's marketing touch. However, much handmade, turn-of-the-century glass has the visual "feel" of the Arts and Crafts Movement without any ties to guild-workshop production methods—appearance alone is not a reliable criterion.

Harry Powell designed glass in imitation of Medieval and Renaissance works, executed by Whitefriars. Some glass manufacturers, like Dorflinger, of White Mills, Pennsylvania, associated their products with Arts and Crafts firms. Stickley catalogues of the 1912–15 era offered Dorflinger glass alongside Craftsman furniture.

Major glass producers the world over, from France's Emile Galle and René Lalique to America's Fenton Art Glass and Durand Art Glass, made objects resembling Arts and Crafts designs, but their ties to the movement are questionable. Fenton Art Glass Company, for example, enlisted a team of skilled European glass artists in 1925 in an effort to emulate Tiffany's commercial success. These same artisans had been employed by other American firms, including Imperial and Durand. Their line was well received and marketed by Fenton for some time. Other production-oriented glass houses, including Imperial Glass Company, ventured into free-blown art glass but never achieved commercial success.

Italy was a notable exception to Arts and Crafts glassmaking innovations for the simple reason that this historic glass center had never departed from the Medieval standards of workmanship and materials set by such centers as Murano. While other artisans sought to return to guildlike teams and medieval techniques, Italian glassmakers went on as they had always done.

Below: Box comprising a basket of silver plate lined with crystal glass, Josef Hoffmann, 1905, executed by the Wiener Werkstätte. *The severe simplicity of this design is characteristic of Arts and Crafts glass work in Austria and the Scandinavian countries.*

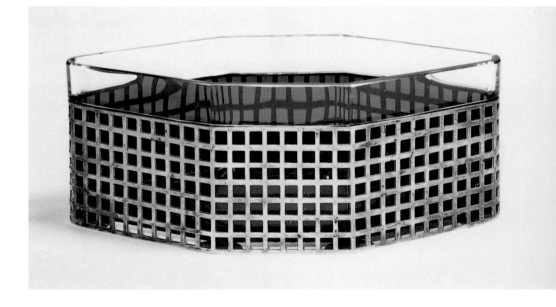

TIFFANY JACK-IN-THE-PULPIT VASE (opposite)

A vivid exemplar of Tiffany's passion for glass and for natural forms, this flower-shaped vase of transparent dark blue glass was heavily iridized to produce the lustrous, rainbow-like color effect. It was produced at Tiffany Studio's Corona, New York, glassworks around 1912.

TIFFANY FLUTED FLOWER-FORM VASE (left)

This delicate blown-glass vase combines colorless, transparent green, and translucent opal iridescent lead glass. It was produced at the Tiffany Studios facility between 1900 and 1905. Louis C. Tiffany inherited a successful jewelry business from his father, Charles Louis Tiffany, but also studied painting under George Innes and in Paris. He was inspired by William Morris and turned to the decorative arts in 1878. Successful in all of his decorating commissions, he achieved his most enduring fame for his work in glass. The unique iridescent colors he achieved were the result of exposing the molten glass to vaporized metals.

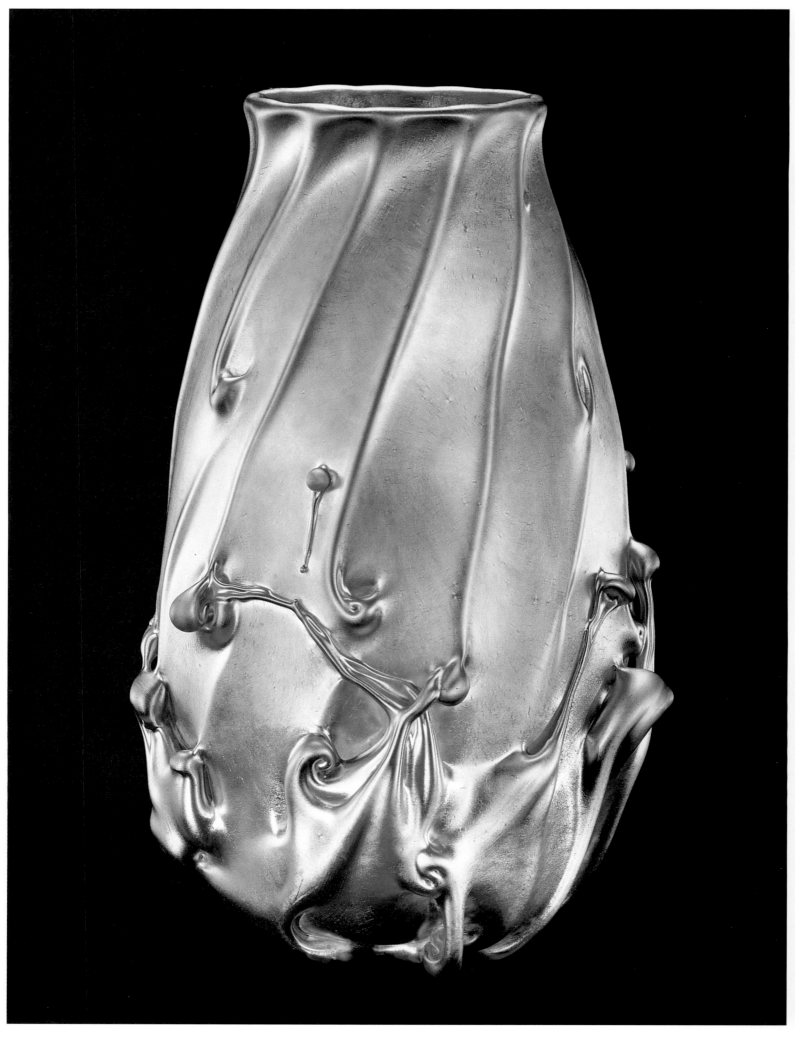

HUNGARIAN IRIDESCENT VASE, IRREGULAR *(above)*

This blown-glass vase was a product of the Hungarian cultural renaissance that began in 1896, with the Millennium Celebrations of Hungary's Magyar origins. The quest for national identity took artists down many new paths, from the revival of folk art to the decoration of Hungarian pavilions for international exhibitions.

CLUTHA VASE, C. 1885–95, GLASGOW *(left)*

Transparent green and amber glasses form this long-necked blown-glass vessel, probably designed by Christopher Dresser for James Cooper & Sons of Glasgow. Dresser was an influential designer and writer on the decorative arts who, like Morris, produced numerous designs for many different household objects.

GOLD AURENE VASE, FREDERICK CARDER *(opposite)*

Produced about 1910 at the Steuben Glass Works in Corning, New York, by cofounder Frederick Carder, this striking vase is formed of transparent amber lead glass, blown and heavily iridized. The Anglo-American designer moved to the United States in 1903 to establish what would become a major glasshouse. He developed this gold metallic luster glass which he patented as Aurene. (Later, Blue Aurene was introduced.)

KEW BLAS IRIDESCENT WINEGLASS *(right)*

The Union Glass Company of Somerville, Massachusetts, produced this iridescent wineglass in the late 19th-early 20th century. The glasshouse was founded in 1851 by Amory and Francis Houghton and reorganized in 1860. It continued to make fine cut and blown glass until 1924.

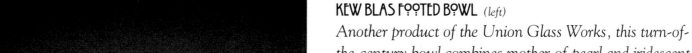

KEW BLAS FOOTED BOWL *(left)*

Another product of the Union Glass Works, this turn-of-the-century bowl combines mother-of-pearl and iridescent glasses in a classical shape enhanced by the curves of the pattern around the base.

TIFFANY FLOWER-FORM LAMP *(left)*

America's premier glassmaker designed this elegant chande-lier-type table lamp with lily-shaped favrile glass shades arch-ing gracefully from the stemlike bronze base. The shades have an amber cast to soften the effect of the lighting.

TIFFANY TABLE LAMP *(left)*

This classic Tiffany design combines a turtleback leaded-glass shade and painted bronze base. The lamp on the front cover, which is in Frank Lloyd Wright's 1908 Meyer May House in Grand Rapids, Michigan, is another example of this signature style.

OTTO PRUTSCHER WINEGLASSES (opposite)

Designed for the firm of E. Bakalowits und Söhne of Vienna, these art-glass goblets were made to Prutscher's design at the Meyr's Neffe factory (Austria/Bohemia) around 1907. The glass on the left comprises colorless and transparent red glasses, blown, cased, cut, and polished.

JOSEF HOFFMANN TABLEWARE, C. 1916 (above)

Blown glass of transparent cobalt blue: a series of vessels produced for Vienna's Wiener Werkstätte to Josef Hoffmann's designs. The harmonious simplicity of this set reflects Hoffmann's stated intention of creating "an island of tranquillity" in domestic design by way of the craft workshop he founded with Koloman Moser.

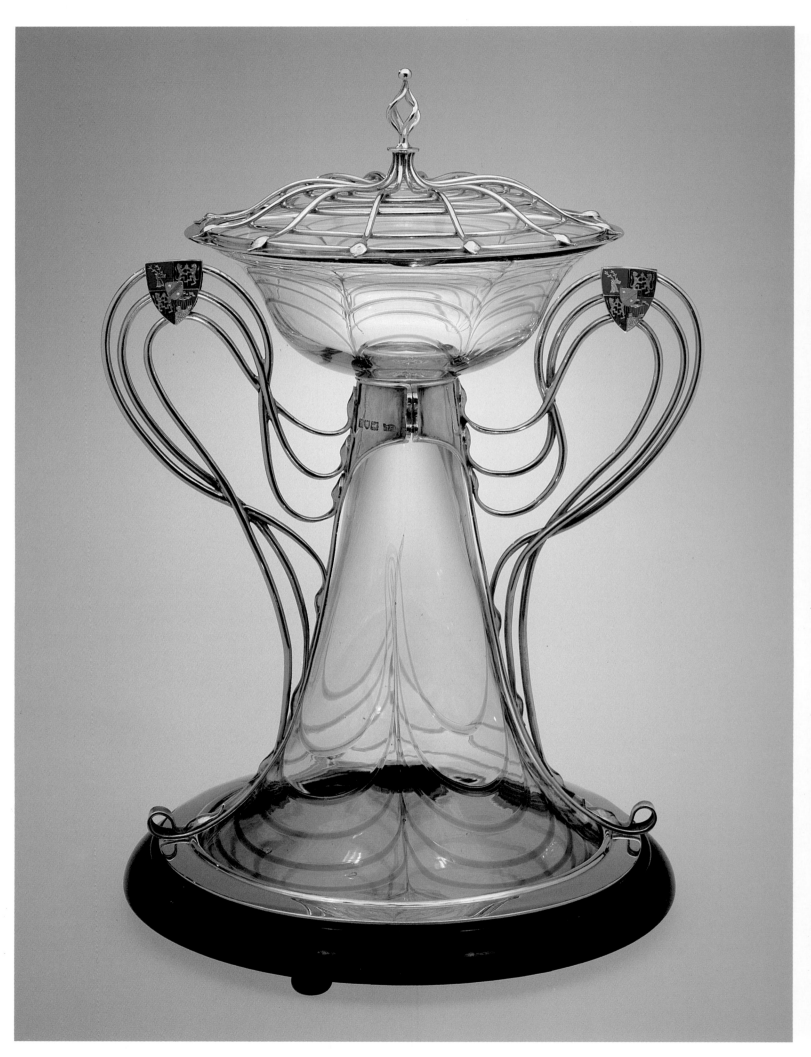

CENTERPIECE, JAMES POWELL & SONS, ENGLAND *(opposite)*
*Commissioned by Count Minerbi in 1906, this elaborate
centerpiece was designed by Harry Powell and executed at
his firm's Whitefriars Glass Works, London. It comprises
colorless and transparent green glasses with trailed and
pulled decoration, blown and mounted in silver and wood,
with enamelled heraldic shields.*

CHRISTOPHER DRESSER DECANTER *(above)*
*This severely simple decanter of colorless glass, blown, cut,
and mounted in electroplated silver with a wooden handle,
was produced during the 1880s by Hukin and Heath, which
had glassmaking facilities at both Birmingham and London.*

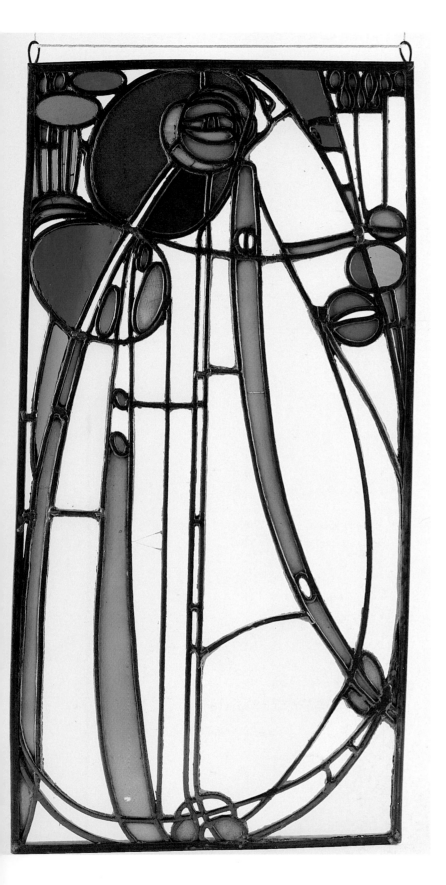

C. R. MACKINTOSH LEADED GLASS PANEL (left)

The architectural quality of this panel helps to identify it as the work of Glasgow designer Charles Rennie Mackintosh, who executed it for the Rose Boudoir featured in the international exhibition at Turin in 1902. The Scottish section of the exhibition was widely acclaimed, enabling Mackintosh to build on his earlier success at the Eighth Secession Exhibition in Vienna.

WILLET STAINED GLASS WINDOWS (opposite)

Stained glass designer and mural painter William Willet produced these Beatrice and Dante windows. He studied and collaborated with John La Farge, set up his own studio in Philadelphia and carried out many ecclesiastical commissions between 1910 and 1920. These included the chapel at West Point Military Academy and Cleveland's Trinity Cathedral. With Ann Lee Willet, he designed the imposing Liberal Arts Window at Princeton University's Proctor Hall (1913).

JOHN LA FARGE WINDOW, C.1897 (opposite)

Designed for the Patrick W. Ford House in Jamaica Plain, Massachusetts, this cut and leaded glass window is a tribute to the artistry of John La Farge, who pioneered new techniques in American glassmaking. Here, colorless, transparent, and translucent polychrome glasses were cut and assembled with lead and plating.

TIFFANY LANDSCAPE WINDOW, C. 1900 (left)

Comprising multicolored blown sheet glass cut into elements and welded together, this decorative window was produced at Tiffany Studio's Corona, Long Island, facility. Note the depth achieved by the gradations of color from bright to dark and the placement of the leading.

CERAMICS

t would be impossible to present a definitive catalogue of Arts and Crafts ceramics within the constraints of a single chapter. Unlike furniture, glassware and metalwork, pottery could be fashioned at home or in a small studio setting, and there were a great many successful Arts and Crafts ceramists. However, the artists and their pieces included here will serve to introduce the major stylistic themes and influences on pottery of the United Kingdom, Europe, and the United States during the period circa 1860–1910.

The design and production of pottery in the United Kingdom during the nineteenth century had expanded with the growth of both cities and population attendant upon the spread of mass-production techniques. These factors had led to a decline in demand for the traditional wares of the skilled potter, which were deemed crudely finished in comparison with factory-made items, while tin and glass containers became popular as more practical and cheaper alternatives. Although the major United Kingdom commercial potteries continued to expand throughout the mid-nineteenth century, streamlining techniques and taking advantage of burgeoning overseas markets, the quality of design deteriorated. The sumptuously decorated porcelain exhibited by such factories as Minton and Worcester at the Great Exhibition of 1851, though technically accomplished, lacked aesthetic harmony.

The Continental exhibitors, especially the French, although they took many prizes, had their critics as well, notably Count Léon de Laborde, who organized the French participants. His report on the exhibition, published in 1856, criticized the obsession with copying the great art of antiquity. He advocated a collaboration among the arts, sciences, and industry whereby artists would involve themselves in enhancing the beauty and integrity of the everyday environment. French architect Eugène Emmanuel Viollet-le-Duc, who taught at the Parisian École des Arts Decoratifs, espoused the views of Ruskin and de Laborde on unity in interior design.

William Morris was one of the first to revive high standards of design and craftsmanship to the medium, collaborating

with perhaps the most prolific and innovative designer of Arts and Crafts ceramics, William De Morgan. While their products were internationally acclaimed, many less well-known artist potters working in studio conditions made their contributions to Arts and Crafts ceramics. These included Aller Vale Pottery, Bretby Art Pottery, Burmantofts, Della Robbia Pottery, Pilkington's Tile & Pottery Co., and W.H. Taylor's Ruskin Pottery. Small local concerns like the Watcombe Pottery, C.H. Brannam, E. Elton, and W. Moorcroft continued to work in local clay, often combining the fashionable with the traditional.

While independent ceramic producers such as Morris and De Morgan were able to control the content and production of their ceramics from start to finish, the larger commercial factories, including Minton and Maw & Company, in their response to the middle-class demand for art tiles, still relied to some extent upon division of labor. In the 1860s Doulton & Company collaborated with the students of Lambeth School of Art, who decorated salt-glazed stoneware made at the Lambeth workshop in London. Doulton provided the blank vessels and the artists were given free rein.

Below: Painted tiles with scenes from the fairy tale Cinderella, *designed by Edward Burne-Jones and executed by Morris and Company, c. 1863–4.*

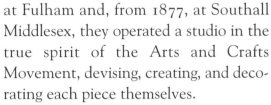

Below: German designer
Max Läuger worked at the
Grand Ducal factory at
Darmstadt and created this
vase in 1900. Most of his
art pottery took a simplified
Oriental form decorated in
a limited range of colors
with stylized flower and
other plant forms. This
piece was much admired at
the turn-of-the-century
Paris International
Exposition.

Hannah and Florence Barlow, with their brother Arthur, are probably the best-known family of decorators working for Doulton's Lambeth studio. Hannah specialized in incised country scenes depicting animals, children, or laborers. The incised decoration was then filled with colored pigment. Florence developed her own style of painting birds and foliage in thick layers of colored slip (thinned clay used for decorating or coating ceramics). Arthur painted softly colored all-over patterns of stylized foliage. Emily Edwards, Frank Butler, Eliza Simmance, and George Tinworth, whose work was known for whimsical plaques of mice, frogs, and small birds, all became highly successful in this field. However, the most famous students of Lambeth Art School were the Martin brothers: Robert Wallace, Walter, and Edwin. For nearly forty years, first

at Fulham and, from 1877, at Southall Middlesex, they operated a studio in the true spirit of the Arts and Crafts Movement, devising, creating, and decorating each piece themselves.

Mintons also opened an art-pottery studio, in Kensington Gore in 1871, which produced mainly faience pieces (earthenware decorated with colorful opaque glazes) under the direction of William Coleman, who himself designed plates and pilgrim bottles decorated with birds, foliage, and female figures. Biscuit pottery was brought down from the Stoke-on-Trent factory and decorated by individual artists. Both Walter Crane, who designed tiles for Maw & Company, and Christopher Dresser worked freelance for Mintons and Wedgwood. Christopher Dresser, possibly the most influential industrial designer of his time, drew upon a vast repertoire of sources, including Greek, Roman, Egyptian, Celtic, Chinese, and Japanese forms and motifs.

Enthusiasm for Japanese forms and glazes was almost universal in pottery and the other decorative arts in the late nineteenth century. The French artist and designer Félix Braquemond and Eugene Rousseau created their own dinner service, inspired by a volume of Hokusai's *Manga*, which was widely admired in Great Britain and the United States.

Among the most influential designers in France during the 1860s and 1870s were Théodore Deck, Ernest Chaplet, Auguste Delaherche, and Taxile Doat, who worked at Sèvres from 1900 on his "*pâte-sur-pâte*" pieces, characterized by medallions applied to porcelain bodies in naturalistic gourd shapes. Deck fashioned brilliant faience with Japanese, Turkish, and Egyptian elements. Initially, Ernest

Chaplet directed the Haviland workshops in Autueil producing barbotine ware — a process of underglaze decoration with colored slips. By contrast, Auguste Delaherche, who bought the Haviland factory from Chaplet in 1887, worked on salt-glaze stoneware from 1883 to 1886, experimenting with the drip glazes he had seen on Japanese stoneware.

As in England and France, Germany had its own independent artisans experimenting with new techniques, as well as modest art potteries using local clays and large commercial potteries such as Meissen and Berlin. Meissen enlisted the assistance of many freelance designers and, spurred on by the work of the Secession potters, produced more innovative lines, commissioning Henry Van der Velde to create tableware to compare with their popular Krokus design service. The factory also cast figures for the sculptor Ernst Barlach.

Max Von Heider and his sons, Hans, Fritz, and Rudolf, worked in Schongau in Bavaria on lustreware, which owed much to the Hungarian Zsolnay factory. As a graduate of the Vienna Polytechnic who had his first success at the Vienna World Exhibition in 1873, Vilmos Zsolnay had considerable influence upon both German and Austrian ceramics.

Many of the Munich Secession artists, and those who worked at the Grand Ducal factory at Darmstadt, including Max Läuger, were also involved in creating ceramic designs. The stylistic influence of both the Symbolist and the Naturalist movements in fine art, with their elongated flowing forms and symbolic bird and animal motifs, can be seen in some of the Continental pottery.

Johann Julius Scharvogel began his career at Villeroy and Boch in 1883 modeling salt-glaze stoneware before moving to Darmstadt. By 1900, when he won a Grand Prix and Gold Medal at the Paris Exhibition, his forms had become simpler, with brightly colored high-temperature glazes in turquoise, red, olive green, and terracotta, in response to the Oriental pottery he had seen while studying in London and Paris.

In Austria, the *Wiener Werkstätte* did not produce its own ceramics until 1916–17; until that time it commissioned such potteries as J. Böck and Wiener Keramik, which was founded in 1905 by Berthold Löffler and Michael Powolny, also a co-founder of the Secession Artists Association. Powolny is best known for his highly distinctive white faience cherubs surrounded by cascades of brightly colored stylized flowers, as well as for his elongated figures. Löffler also produced figures in a similar style as well as tectonic tableware in monochrome. Both Powolny and Löffler taught classes in ceramics at the influential Vienna *Kunstgewerbeschule*, while Kolo Moser and Josef Hoffmann taught design.

At the turn of the nineteenth century, Dutch ceramics were highly inventive. A. C. Colenbrander created eggshell earthenware for the Rozenburg pottery in the Hague and, later, for

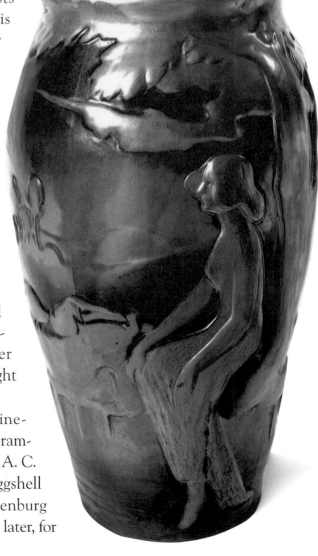

Below: *The Hungarian Pécs Pottery, taken over from his father by Vilmos Zsolnay in 1853, produced this graceful vase with pensive seated figure. Zsolnay's designs made Pécs a commercial success, with 1,000 employees by 1900.*

Right: A group of vessels and a decorative tile from Rookwood Pottery, Cincinnati, Ohio. The pottery's decorative wares became increasingly sophisticated from its foundation in 1880 by Maria Longworth Nichols to its most vigorous period, c. 1890–1920.

the Ram pottery at Arnhem. Both his work and Juriaan Kok's, emulated at the Wed. N. Brantjes factory at Purmerend, is eccentric in form, with flamelike distortions and elongations.

The development of Scandinavian design is unique in that Denmark and Sweden had their own long history of independent and immediately recognizable style. In Sweden, the Rörstrand and Gustavsberg factories were the most important. It was Alf Wallander, a painter and ceramic designer, who led the way in Swedish Art Nouveau in the applied arts at the Rörstrand factory, as a designer from 1895 and art director in 1900. He manufactured mainly delicate underglaze-painted porcelain with relief decoration of plant forms.

The leading light of Danish pottery was Thorvald Bindesbøll, working in stylized cloud and wave forms in earthy colors taken from his own watercolors. These were outlined in *sgraffito* (scratching through a surface glaze to reveal a different color underneath) on rustic earthenware plates and vases. Pietro Krøhn was the other great Danish ceramicist. At Bing & Grøndahl, he produced some superb tableware, including decorative cups in flower and leaf shapes as well as his famous Heron Service, in porcelain with molded decoration, painted in vibrant underglaze blue. Copenhagen's connoisseurs, including Arnold Krog, art director at Royal Copenhagen, were fascinated by Japanese arts and crafts. Contemporary writings on the heron and crane decorations of Japanese scrolls may have been the inspiration for his service.

Finland, after it gained political independence from Russia in 1917, sought to create its own identity free from Swedish influence. Thus there is something incongruous in the fact that its most significant ceramics decorator was Alfred Finch, an Anglo-Belgian. He became involved with the Arts and Crafts Movement during a visit to England, and after working at Boch Frères was invited to Finland by Louis Sparre, who was setting up his Iris workshops. Finch's work was simple in

design, decorated in wave patterns in colored slip glazes with the occasional use of incised motifs. The effect was a simplicity and harmony of form and decoration of which any of the 1851 Great Exhibition critics would have been proud.

Twenty-five years after the original dissension about the quality of design in England, the argument was raging again, this time at the Centennial Exposition of 1876 in Philadelphia, where Japanese arts and crafts captured the public imagination. Doulton exhibited examples of its salt-glaze stoneware and underglaze-painted earthenware from the Lambeth studio, and Chaplet's barbotine slipware. American pottery was being compared with European and British examples and found lacking. Isaac Broome fumed that there was "nothing to approach even the lower grades of European ware." It was feared that the United States would be dubbed a backwoods colony. However, there was at least one strength on the American side. The Cincinnati Room in the Women's Pavilion displayed samples

of mineral painting on china over glaze, carried out by a small circle of amateur painters from Ohio. Traditionally, ceramics had been regarded as a worthy pastime for middle-class ladies at home; now it seemed possible that a woman could be gainfully employed outside the home without losing her status as a lady. Ruskin's freedom through labor took on a whole new significance in the female domain.

It was Mary Louise McLaughlin who, having exhibited some of her own blue-on-white china painting at the 1876 Exposition, and encouraged by the new developments she had seen, started producing her own slip-decorated wares and her Cincinnati Limoges glaze (later renamed Cincinnati Faience) about 1877. This involved painting in a slip of unfired clay mixed with mineral pigments on a damp earthenware body. In 1879 McLaughlin formed the Cincinnati Pottery Club to continue her experiments in the company of like-minded friends. In 1901 she produced a high-temperature, trans-

Right: *Glaze detail,
Weller/Sicard, Zanesville,
Ohio. The three influential
art potteries in the city of
Zanesville, of which
Samuel A. Weller's (1896)
was the best known, were
quick to respond to public
demand for matte glazes.
This piece (shown on
page 90) is a relatively
rare example of high relief
modelling.*

lucent, cream-colored ware she called Losanti. This was decorated with trailing plant designs or perforated and filled in with glaze. Her palette of glazes included delicate pastel blues and peach with green highlights.

Throughout the 1870s underglaze decoration became the new standard for American art pottery. The Chelsea Keramic Art Works was founded in 1872 by James Robertson and his sons, George Hugh and Alexander. In 1877 Chelsea faience was

introduced, as well as barbotine ware using colored slips to decorate on a green or blue base. In 1884, Hugh Robertson developed his *sang de boeuf* glaze. After a major financial crisis that threatened closure, the pottery moved to new premises as Dedham Pottery. The real success here was the popular line of crackle-glaze tableware with blue "in-glaze" borders of flowers, ducks, and rabbits.

So great was the impact of the Centennial Exposition that a crop of more than thirty potteries shot up in the state of Ohio alone. The most famous of these was the Rookwood Pottery in Cincinnati, established by Maria Longworth Nichols Storer in 1880 with support from her father and some of the women at the Cincinnati Pottery Club. Nichols allowed the club to use the Rookwood premises until 1882. Rookwood's Standard Ware consisted of brown, yellow, and orange flowers or figures painted in slip under glaze on grounds of varying shades of ochre. Individual artists were allowed to develop their own styles; some went on to set up their own potteries, including

Right: *Marblehead
(Massachusetts) Pottery
group showing the firm's
characteristic simple
shapes, conventionalized
decoration, and subtly colored matte glazes. The
pottery originated as an
occupational therapy workshop for patients at Dr.
Herbert Hall's sanatarium
in 1904.*

Albert Valentin and Artus Van Briggle. Rookwood's main rival was William H. Grueby Co. of Boston, especially after its development of a matte glaze. The company was incorporated into Grueby Faience & Tile Company in 1891 and provided L.F. Tiffany with lamp bases for his glass shades.

Technical and artistic inventions were introduced to Zanesville, Ohio, potteries between 1902 and 1904 by Frederick H. Rhead, an Englishman who introduced a technique at the Weller Pottery whereby outlines of decoration were piped in white slip onto a grey or blue ground and filled in with a contrasting color. Rhead also initiated the Della Robbia line of pottery at the Roseville Pottery at Zanesville using a *sgraffito* technique.

It was a time of great innovation, aesthetically, technically, and socially. Women's education was being taken seriously. Newcomb College in New Orleans (1895), University City Pottery in St. Louis, Missouri (1907), and the Paul Revere Pottery in Boston (1906), with its Saturday Evening Girls' Club, were set up to train women in the artistic and technical side of ceramics, although the throwing of pots was still usually done by men.

Some of the potteries seem to have began almost by accident. Particularly curious was the way in which the Pewabic Pottery was established. Horace James Caulkins was a ceramicist who worked as a dental supplier. With Mary Perry, he designed a gas-fired kiln that was taken up by a number of art potteries. In 1904 the pair set up the Pewabic Pottery, with Caulkins as the clay technician and Perry designing and glazing the pottery. Teco was originally set up in 1880 as the American Terra Cotta & Ceramic Co. for the

manufacture of drainpipes. However, after some success with experiments at art pottery in 1895, they started to market it under the now familiar name. The Marblehead Pottery also had an unusual start, as therapy for patients suffering from nervous exhaustion. It became independent of the medical project in 1905 under the artistic direction of A.E. Baggs, becoming another Arts and Crafts institution whose origins were more philanthropic than artistic.

One pottery seems, like the Martin Bros. in England, to embrace the ethos of the Arts & Crafts Movement and to epitomize the American art potter. George E. Ohr's Biloxi Art Pottery, in Mississippi, was a family business that manufactured a vast array of eccentric shapes and designs while absorbing new ideas from many sources. Ohr did everything himself while drawing inspiration from the world around him. The success of the American art potters transcended their assimilation of developments in Great Britain and Europe: in the transformative heat of their own kilns, they were able to create their own unique art.

Left: Vase from the Saturday Evening Girls Club (Paul Revere Pottery), Boston. The social mission of the arts found expression in this ceramic studio, founded to provide employment opportunities for poor girls from primarily Italian and Jewish immigrant families. Designs were based on simple floral and figural patterns outlined in black or incised and filled with flat, naturalistic tones.

CHRISTOPHER DRESSER EARTHENWARE VASE *(above)*

From 1892 onward, Dresser's designs for William Ault's pottery at Swadlincote, England, were increasingly expressive of his own invention, as in this vessel with molded decoration in the form of goats' heads. His wide knowledge of the art of ancient civilizations, including pre-Columbian, Moorish, and Indian, enriched his design repertoire throughout his career.

DE MORGAN TILE PANEL, LION RAMPANT *(opposite)*

William De Morgan's inspiration for tile designs came from English Delft, early Italian majolica, medieval bestiaries, heraldry, and the fantastic creatures of his own imagination. His decorative style was strongly influenced by 14th- and 15th-century Islamic designs, with their palette of so-called Persian colors: blues, turquoise, greens, and reds.

WALTER CRANE GLAZED VASE *(above)*

English painter, designer, and book illustrator Walter Crane (1845–1915) was a devotee of William Morris and well known for his textiles and wallpapers. This glazed vase with its unusual all-over design reflects the influence of both Morris and Art Nouveau.

MARTIN BROTHERS' STONEWARE JUGS *(left)*

The three Martin brothers were best known for their eccentric salt-glazed renderings of grotesque bird figures like these stoneware tobacco jars on wood plinths. They also produced humorous "face jugs," for which Robert Wallace was largely responsible. Known as Wallace, he did most of the firm's modeling, while Walter was engaged in throwing the pots. Edwin's forte was for decoration and the production of miniatures.

DOULTON, LAMBETH: VASES AND BOWL *(above)*

Established manufacturers like Doulton sought new markets in the late 1800s by establishing art potteries, of which the Lambeth Workshop was a successful example. Designer F. C. Pope produced the stoneware vase with greenish glaze and lizard decoration about 1905. He started at Doulton in 1880 and produced consistently individual pieces throughout his long career, with the natural world a major source of inspiration.

JACQUES SICARD RELIEF VASES *(above)*
*Frenchman Jacques Sicard designed these handsome vases
with their iridescent glazes for Samuel A. Weller of
Zanesville, Ohio, as part of his Sicardo ware line, made
c. 1900–07. Sicard was influenced by French art potters
such as Auguste Delaherche and Ernest Chaplet who
developed experimental glazes in the late 19th century.*

FRENCH PAINTED EARTHENWARE DISH (below)

Joseph-Théodore Deck produced this plate decorated by Emmanuel Benner at his studio in Paris about 1865. Deck employed painters and designers of the highest caliber, including Felix Braquemond. Both Emmanuel Benner and his twin brother Jean worked with Deck regularly and were kindred spirits in their enthusiasm for Japanese motifs.

DOAT SÈVRES PORCELAIN VASE, C. 1900 *(above)*

Taxile Maximin Doat joined the Sèvres factory in 1877 and became its principal exponent of Pâte-sur-pâte work, especially medallions applied to porcelain bodies, as on this vase decorated with the heads of the goddesses Juno, Venus, and Minerva.

SÈVRES BISCUIT PORCELAIN FIGURINE *(right)*

This elegant figurine is one of a group of fifteen entitled Jeu de L'Echarpe, modeled by Agathon Léonard. The group was part of the Sèvres exhibit at the 1900 Paris Exhibition, at which the acclaimed porcelain house won a Grand Prix. The American dancer Lole Fuller, who appeared in Paris in 1893, probably served as the inspiration for this much-copied group.

KROG PORCELAIN VASE, CRYSTALLINE GLAZE (above)

Designed by Arnold Krog for the Royal Copenhagen Porcelain Factory around 1900. Krog was a versatile painter and ceramist who was also an architect. As art director at the Royal Copenhagen Porcelain Factory (from 1885) he revived the soft muted-blue underglaze painting for which the factory had been known in the late 18th century. He also developed various crystalline glazes for commercial production.

DANISH PORCELAIN VASE PAINTED BY RODE (opposite)

The Royal Copenhagen Porcelain Factory also produced this vase entitled Strandtidsel(Sea Holly), with painted decoration in underglaze colors by Gottfried Rode.

DUTCH EARTHENWARE DISH, PAINTED *(below)*

Produced at Weduwe NSA Brantjes & Company, Purmerend, Holland, about 1900. The factory was founded in 1895 by Petronella Clementine van Rijn, the widow of Nicolaas Brantjes. After initial production of traditional Delftware, the factory began to create more contemporary designs in the mode of the Rozenburg Pottery in the Hague and De Porcelayne Fles, combining eccentric flamelike forms with dense, intricate floral decoration.

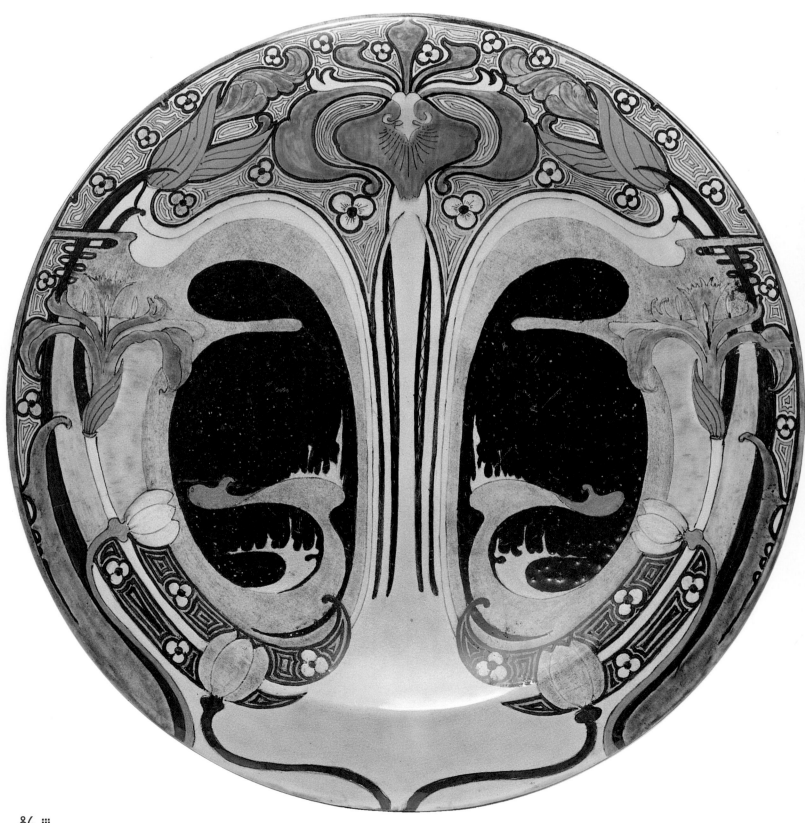

FINNISH EARTHENWARE BOWL AND MUG (above)

This set was produced in the Iris Workshops at Parvoo about 1900. The decoration was cut through colored slip by Alfred William Finch. The Iris (later Iris/Finch) Workshops were founded by the Swede Louis Sparre and the Finnish painter Akseli Gallen-Kallela to promote a new national spirit in design. In 1897 Sparre met English-born Alfred Finch, who had been brought up in Brussels and studied at its Academy of Art. As head of the ceramics studio at Iris, he experimented with high-fired glazes and decoration comprising incised lines, flowing wavelike patterns, and contrasting spots of slip.

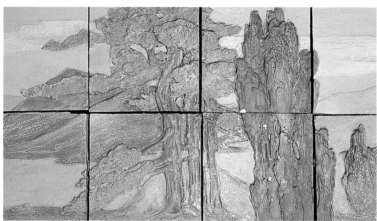

ROOKWOOD POTTERY VASES, CINCINNATI, OHIO (opposite)
Japanese artist Kataro Shirayamadani joined Rookwood in 1887 and remained until his death in 1948. His work had a strong influence on the company, which produced only decorative wares—primarily painted with floral and plant motifs. One of Rookwood's major innovations was the application of pastel-colored slip by atomizer under a high-gloss or matte glaze to produce the successful line called "Rookwood Standard."

ROOKWOOD EARTHENWARE, PAINTED AND INCISED (above)
Rookwood was known for its rich green and brown glazes, including the "tiger-eye" crystalline glaze introduced in 1884. Most Rookwood pottery was painted by such artists as Laura Anne Fry, Matthew Andrew Daly, and Lenore Asbury. Incised and relief designs like those at center could be painted in different colors from the body, emphasized by relief modeling, or highlighted by electrodeposited metal.

AMERICAN ART POTTERY TILES, VARIOUS (above)
English-inspired portrait tiles, top (from U.S. Encaustic, Low Art Tile Works, Beaver Falls, and Kensington); Rookwood tile frieze, center; and "Autumn" plaque by Herman Mueller.

CHELSEA KERAMIC ART WORKS VASES *(below)*

Hugh C. Robertson's art pottery, founded with Charles Volkmar in Massachusetts (1872), used all the decorative techniques that had been developed over the previous twenty years, as seen in the left-hand vase with its landscape medallion and high-relief modeling. However, his primary concern was in producing simple stoneware bodies in Chinese-type monochrome glazes (oxblood example at right): he experimented for years at great expense but with unrivaled results

GEORGE OHR ART POTTERY, BILOXI *(above)*

George E. Ohr founded his Biloxi, Mississippi, art pottery in the early 1880s, hauling clay from nearby rivers and throwing his pots on a homemade wheel. He was a genuine eccentric who experimented with many techniques, including pinching, ruffling, and twisting the bodies of his vessels, which were fired at low temperatures in a wood-fired kiln. His family helped in the business, and he described himself modestly as "the greatest art potter on the earth," hawking his wares at regional trade fairs.

OHR VASE, CURLING RIBBON HANDLES *(left)*

This vase with tapering neck and bulbous top has an accordion-like snake applied under the finish, which shades from metallic green to splotchy rose. Ohr's quirky creations were not highly marketable, and when a customer did come to the pottery to purchase his wares, Ohr often chased after him to retrieve a beloved piece. The saying in Biloxi was, "Only the fleet own George Ohr pottery."

NEWCOMB COLLEGE POTTERY VASE, NEW ORLEANS *(right)*

Early high-glazed scenic vase with carved oak trees, a frequent motif drawn from local vegetation, which included wisteria, syringa, orange blossom, palm trees, and conifers. The pottery opened at the Sophie Newcomb Memorial College for Women (affiliated with Tulane University) in 1895. Directed by Ellsworth Woodward, the pottery developed a distinctive style using a process by which designs were incised onto sponged unfired local clay. After firing, underglaze oxides were applied in a palette of blue, green, yellow, and black before application of a high-gloss transparent glaze.

NEWCOMB COLLEGE AND GRUEBY POTTERY VASES *(below)*

(Left) Newcomb College vase decorated by Maria LeBlanc; (right) Grueby Pottery vase with five scrolled handles and tall spiked leaves under characteristic matte green finish (Florence Liley).

GRUEBY POTTERY VASE, G. P. KENDRICK *(left)*

This eleven-inch-tall vase with rolled rim was decorated by Ruth Erickson with long broad leaves alternating with sharply defined yellow buds. It was produced at William H. Grueby's successful Grueby Faience Company, founded in 1897 in Boston to make ceramic art wares. George P. Kendrick designed the vessels, whose organic forms and matte glazes show the influence of Auguste Delaherche. The well-known "Grueby Green" glaze, with its ribbed, speckled finish, resembling cucumber skin, was emulated by many other potteries.

GRUEBY BOWL, FLARING RIM *(below)*

This broad bowl was decorated by Annie Lingley with yellow five-petaled blossoms alternating between double rows of rounded leaves. Grueby wares were popularized by Gustav Stickley, who used them in his interiors.

GRUEBY ARCHITECTURAL TILE *(left)*

From 1892, William H. Grueby produced ceramic tile like the example at left, depicting a Spanish galleon in the deep cuenca first used by Spanish tilemakers. Grueby had learned tile ceramics at the J. & J. G. Low tileworks during his teens and produced them for the Revere Pottery.

TIFFANY STUDIOS ART POTTERY AND GLAZE DETAIL (*above and right*)
Louis C. Tiffany unveiled the art pottery he called "Favrile Old Ivory" at the 1904 St. Louis Exposition, after six years of experimentation. A white clay was used for this line, which was cast in molds and fired at high temperature to produce an off-white glaze before hand finishing. Over time, crystalline, matte, and iridescent glazes were added to production, and in 1911 "Favrile Bronze" pottery, with electroplated and patined metal coatings, was introduced, probably in response to Clewell Metal Art Wares.

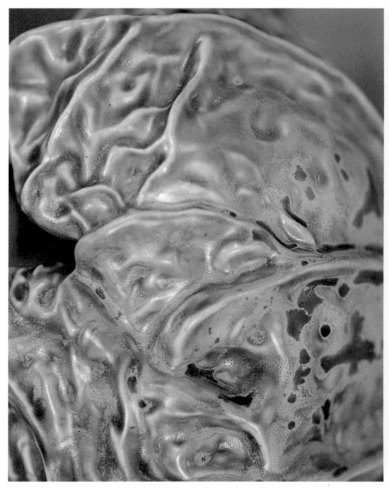

FULPER POTTERY GROUP *(above)*

Clockwise from left: Tall vase; large two-handled footed urn glazed in striated green matte crystalline glaze over "hammered" surface; tall flaring cylinder vase in rich green textured semi-gloss over ivory crystalline flambe; tapering vase with large ring handles, moss green to rose flambe glaze; bulbous vase with wishbone handles, matte green finish over "hammered" surface; scalloped open bowl glazed with medium-green to ivory interior; artichoke bowl with concentric rows of spiked leaves, medium-green flowing flambe over mahogany-brown flambe; ibis bowl with three winged birds, glazed with emerald-green crystalline interior and feathered blue-green-over-mahogany exterior.

FULPER VASEKRAFT LAMP *(left)*

In 1909 New Jersey's venerable Fulper Pottery (founded in 1814 as the Samuel Hill Pottery) began producing its Vasekraft line, including specially glazed bowls, lamps, bookends, and other Arts and Crafts wares.

TECO SHORT-NECKED VASE *(right)*

"Teco" was the short-form name for the popular line of moderately priced art pottery produced by American Terra Cotta & Ceramic Co./Gates Potteries, founded at Terra Cotta, Illinois, by William D. Gates in 1880. From 1901, art pottery was made from molded or thrown local clays. This example has a long cylindrical body flowing downward to an open-swirling leaf base, covered in rich matte green to slightly grayish glaze.

TECO VASE, FLORAL MOTIF *(below)*

Petals, leaves, and water plants, both molded and applied, figured largely in Teco's art pottery. Prominent Prairie-school architects, including Frank Lloyd Wright and William J. Dodd, were invited to submit designs to the Midwestern firm.

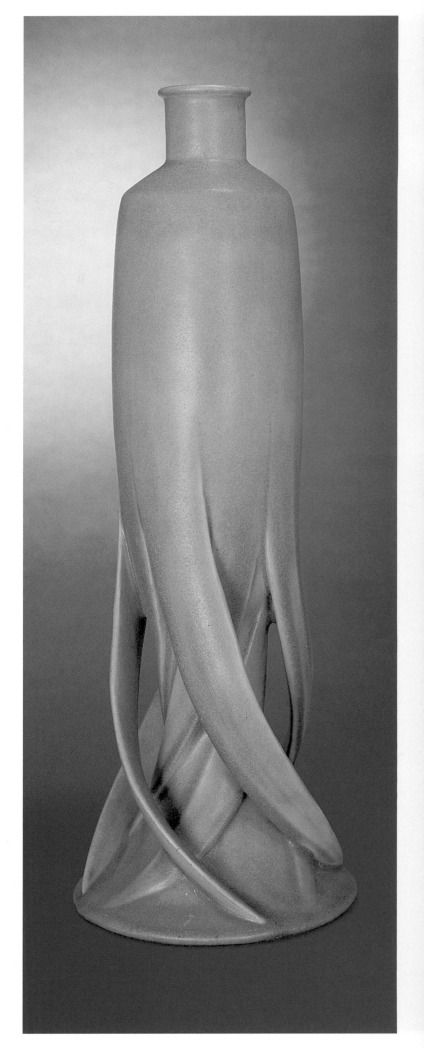

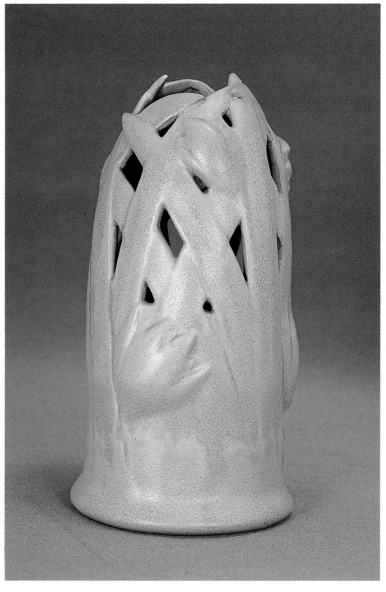

SOUTHWESTERN ART POTTERY GROUP *(left)*

The rear and center right pieces in this group were produced by Artus Van Briggle. They show the sculptural quality typical of his work, due in part to his studies in Paris for Rookwood. In the early 1900s, he relocated to Colorado Springs to be treated for tuberculosis and set up the Van Briggle Pottery Company to produce hand-finished molded pottery. After his death in 1904, his wife, Anne Gregory Van Briggle, took over the business successfully.

PEWABIC POTTERY GROUP *(below)*

Michigan's Pewabic Pottery, founded by Horace J. Caulkin and Mary Chase Perry, produced this group designed by Perry, whose interest in glazes led to progressively simpler forms and experimentation with contrasting iridescent and luster glazes. The pottery took its Chippewa Indian name from the local copper-colored clay and a Michigan river. Collector Charles L. Freer helped make Perry's work widely known, and she has become well represented in American museums.

METALWORK

hroughout the nineteenth century, the city of Birmingham, England, enjoyed a somewhat dubious reputation for the mass production of cheap, poorly made jewelry and brassware. Nevertheless, there was a strong belief within the city that education in the arts could help improve the standards of industrial output. This resulted in the Birmingham School of Design, founded in 1843. The school moved to new quarters in Margaret Street in 1888 and was frequently visited by William Morris and Edward Burne-Jones. During the 1890s, headmaster Edward R. Taylor introduced the teachings of Ruskin and Morris with far-reaching effects. From Birmingham's innovative school emerged Joseph Southall (1861–1944), who would lead the revival in tempera painting; Charles Gere (1869–1957) who began his career at the Kelsmscott Press and designed the frontispiece for Morris's *News from Nowhere*; and Arthur Joseph Gaskin (1862–1928) an illustrator of fairy tales and the Kelmscott Press's *The Shepherds' Calendar*, who turned to jewelry design in 1899. In collaboration with his wife Georgina Cave France (1868–1934), Gaskin produced finely worked silver-wire filigree set with cabochon-cut amethysts and mother-of-pearl.

At the turn of the century, Alexander Fisher (1864–1936) fostered a revival in the art of enamelling. His work and his contributions to *The Studio* magazine promoted painted enamel as a jewel or art object, with settings of gold, silver, bronze, and even steel. Often based on Renaissance models, Fisher's jewelry was designed to be worn with the simpler, more comfortable fashions favored by the women of the Arts and Crafts Movement.

Although the art of enamelling was a Guild of Handicrafts medium, it became associated primarily with women either as a hobby or as a profession. In England, some of the best work was produced by Edith Dawson, Phoebe Stabler, Georgina Gaskin, and Phoebe Traquair. In the United States, too, women led the field in jewelry design and manufacture. Elizabeth E. Copeland (1866–1957) is best known for boxes that recall the jewelled and enamelled reliquaries of the Middle Ages; she was a medal winner at both the 1915 Panama-Pacific Exposition and the 1916 Boston Society of Arts and Crafts Exhibition. Mildred G. Watkins (1883–1968) was one of several gifted artists in the Cleveland, Ohio, group that included Ruth Smedley, Mary Blakeslee, Carolyn Hadlow, and Anna Wyers. Watkins first worked with Frances Barnum and Jane Carson, with whom she produced a metalwork and jewelry exhibit for the 1904 Louisiana Purchase Exposition. In 1907 Watkins joined the Boston Society of Arts

Below: The Wagner Buckle (1896) by British jeweler Alexander Fisher: steel with enamel plaques depicting the story of Tristan and Isolde. It is part of a larger piece, The Wagner Girdle, that measures 21½ x 7⅞".

and Crafts, where she was awarded the title of Master Craftsman. Although she continued to collaborate with Cleveland craftsmen and -women in what had become the nation's leading city in this art, Watkins also worked and exhibited independently. Her jewelry, boxes, and small tableware won important prizes for enamelled metalwork.

The English Arts and Crafts Movement produced many distinguished metalsmiths like W.A.S Benson, who opened small workshops and translated the movement's philosophy into industrial production of inexpensive domestic goods. A founder of the Art Workers' Guild, Benson designed hollowware, lampshades, and electrical fixtures. His work, often featured in *The Studio*, was sold in his own Bond Street showroom and at Samuel Bing's Paris shop, L'Art Nouveau. Other metalworkers who set up studios or became teachers at the new schools of art included Henry Wilson (1864–1934), who designed the great bronze doors of the Episcopal Cathedral of St. John the Divine in New York City (1905); jeweller Alexander Fisher (1864–1936), who combined the talents of

goldsmith, painter, and sculptor; and Sir George James Frampton, creator of the statue of Peter Pan in Kensington Gardens. All of these artists became associated with the London Central School of Arts and Crafts. During the 1890s, mainly through the impetus of the Birmingham School of Design's metalwork department, that city became a flourishing center for this craft. The Guild of Handicrafts, with the motto "By Hammer and Hand," was founded by Arthur Dixon (1856–1929), a silversmith trained as an architect. Dixon designed a cathedral in Seoul, Korea, and the guild's headquarters in Great Charles Street, Birmingham. Like Benson, he accepted the use of machinery for constructional components in the interest of "scientific accuracy." The guild's pieces were generally simple in shape, often executed in base metals, with decoration limited to hammered surfaces that were lightly, rather than brilliantly, polished. Base metals like copper came out of the kitchen to be transformed by Arts and Crafts metalworkers. Copper's ductility and malleability made it more workable than precious metals, and it could be colored and patined at a fraction of the cost of gold or silver. Even amateur craftsmen could work it, and

Left: Pendant and chain, Nelson and Edith Dawson, c. 1900: Nelson Dawson crafted this setting of gold and silver gilt, with drops of opal and amethyst, for Edith Dawson's enamelled floral plaque. The Dawsons were among several British couples, including Harold and Phoebe Stabler, who specialized in enamelled metalwork.

Right: *Graceful and durable period metalware, including a copper vase inlaid with silver in a cattail motif and a vase in a copper mount. Many such articles are still in daily use among private collectors.*

in the hands of skillful professionals, copper lamps, bowls, and tea and coffee services became highly distinctive.

Arthur Lasenby Liberty (1843–1917), who founded the decorative arts firm of Liberty & Company, was shrewd enough to see the commercial potential of Arts and Crafts design. Rejecting idealistic concerns about handcrafting, Liberty blended the skills of the craftsman-designer with manufacturing techniques that resulted in the production of more affordable goods of a high quality. The success of Liberty's venture ensured a wider public awareness of Arts and Crafts principles. (Liberty's policy precluded signed work, so most of his designers and craftsmen remained anonymous until a revival of interest in the period encouraged research into their identities.) Liberty's financial success enabled him to commission designs from almost any artist or craftsman, including many Arts and Crafts masters. Designers for Liberty and Co. included Archibald Knox (1864–1933), whose imagination fired the company's Celtic Revival; Jessie M. King (1873–1949), who helped design and decorate C.R. Mackintosh's Scottish Pavilion at the 1902 *Exposizione Nazionale* in Turin; the metalware firm of W. H. Haseler; and Rex Silver (1879–1965), the designer of both Tudric and Cymric Art Nouveau metalware, who also supervised production at the Silver Studio of design founded by his father. In addition to metalwork, Silver also supplied Liberty with some of its most successful textile designs, including the famous Peacock Feather design relaunched in 1975 to mark the firm's centenary. The studio produced some 30,000 designs for decorative art objects over its 83-year history.

The metalware produced for Liberty by W.H. Haseler aroused the anger of C.R. Ashbee, who felt his own work had been plagiarized and degraded. He resented such deviations from Arts and Crafts practice as the addition of hand-wrought hammering to the surface of metal pieces that had, in fact, been manufactured entirely from die-stamped sheets already complete with ornament. Liberty's commercial success did, indeed, contribute to the gradual decline of Ashbee's own Guild of Handicraft during the early 1900s. While it flourished, however, Ashbee's guild was the model for many such organizations abroad, including the Boston Society of Arts and Crafts, Chicago's Hull House, and Ralph Radcliffe Whitehead's Byrdcliffe community near Woodstock, New York. Elbert Hubbard's Roycroft community in East Aurora,

New York, had its own metal shop before 1900 and became well known under the leadership of Karl Kipp, a former banker and self-taught craftsman who eventually supervised 35 artisans and a product line of more than 150 items. Metalworkers at Gustav Stickley's Craftsman Workshops in Eastwood, New York, produced hand-wrought hinges, key escutcheons, and handles for Craftsman furniture, along with fireplace hoods and tools, tableware, desk sets, and other accessories. In Chicago, Clara Pauline Barck established the Kalo Arts and Crafts Community in 1900; it thrived as the city's leading producer of handcrafted silver for several decades.

Austria's Josef Hoffmann, founder of the *Wiener Werkstätte*, encouraged the use of modest materials in metalwork, including plate and sheet metals for tableware and semiprecious stones for jewelry. Unlike the Ashbee-style communities, machine techniques were employed by the *Werkstätte* and its licenced manufacturers. Despite the modest materials and efficient techniques, its products were expensive, made to high standards from good designs. Hoffmann's collaboration with German designers and manufacturers in the *Deutscher Werkbund* became a greater influence on German industrial design than on the hand-craftsmen and artists of the Arts and Crafts Movement. The Scandinavian countries led Europe's fine Arts and Crafts metalwork design and handcrafting. Foremost among these was Denmark's distinguished silversmith Georg Jensen (1866–1935), who designed pieces that ranged from simple geometric hollowware to classic textural and sculptural jewelry. Jensen's work has influenced modern design to the present day.

ROYCROFT COPPER TRAY, DETAIL, C. 1910 (right)

The Copper Shop at Roycroft was originally set up to produce metal hinges for the community's furniture, but it soon diversified into a variety of metalware items like this beaten copper tray, whose sturdy handle joint exemplifies the Arts and Crafts aesthetic of revealed construction. At Roycroft, "honest art" took in many objects for everyday use, including housewares of wrought iron, pewter, and brass.

GUSTAV STICKLEY COPPER TRAY (below)

Apart from surface hammering, motifs from nature were often the sole ornament of base metalware of the period. The curving lines of fruits, flowers, and vines wove a common thread between British and American Arts and Crafts designers.

PERIOD COAL SCUTTLE, FIREWOOD BOX, AND ANDIRON

(above and right)

For period architects, the fireplace was pre-eminent, "the heart of the home," and the kitchen became more important as fewer households kept servants. Handsome stove and fireplace accessories were produced by many Arts and Crafts metalsmiths, including the Roycroft Shops who produced the andirons at right; the Craftsman Workshops; the Art Metal Company of Los Angeles, which worked on commissions from the architects Charles and Henry Greene; and Dirk van Erp's San Francisco studio.

PERIOD COPPER TRAY, CANDLESTICK, AND JUG *(above)*

These pieces show the characteristic hammer marks, patinas, and simplified shapes of Arts and Crafts metal housewares. Note the naturalistic repoussé design on the tray, formed by hammering and pressing on the reverse side to achieve patterns in relief. Many craftsmen, some of whose names did not become well known, produced such pieces. They appear to best advantage in the context of an Arts and Crafts setting, complemented by period textiles, mellow wood furniture, amber-shaded lamps, and simple pottery.

ROYCROFT COPPER VASE WITH SILVER INLAY *(right)*

The geometric piercing at the top of this unusually shaped vase is echoed in the inlay and softened by the overall mottled patina. Many different "antique" effects could be achieved by artificial oxidation and other chemical processes used to patine period copper or its alloys, such as bronze. This type of vase is most effective with unstudied arrangements of tall field flowers and roadside plants like Queen Anne's Lace, burdock, and goldenrod.

ROYCROFT BOX, HAMMERED COPPER *(below)*

The geometric theme is repeated here in the rivetlike studs and the oblong shape, tapering up from the base. The slightly convex lid gives the look of a miniature chest. The overall effect is one of sturdiness and strength rather than artificial elegance—a hallmark of the Arts and Crafts style.

KESWICK SCHOOL PITCHER, C. 1890 *(above)*
Produced at England's Keswick School of Industrial Art,
this copper pitcher shows the refinement that could be
achieved in base metalwork with proper instruction and
materials. As Arts and Crafts spokesman Walter Crane put
it, the movement's mission was to "turn our artists into
craftsmen and our craftsmen into artists."

CLARET JUG, GREAT BRITAIN *(above)*
Some of the most attractive Arts and Crafts objects com-
bined metalwork mounts and glass, as in this claret jug with
its bamboo motif, showing the influence of Far Eastern art
on the movement aesthetic. The London hallmark is 1882.

ARCHIBALD KNOX TEA SERVICE (opposite top)

A native of the Isle of Man, Archibald Knox was a gifted silversmith whose work found wide commercial acceptance. From 1898 he designed much of the Celtic Revival pewter- and silverware for Liberty's of London.

SILVER AND WOOD TEAPOT, C. 1915 (opposite bottom)

This monogrammed piece is attributed to American silversmith Emery W. Todd, who left Chicago's Kalo Shop, founded by Clara Barck Welles, to establish his own Midwestern firm, the TC Shop. Its trademark designs were rounded and organic, as seen in the gracefully curved spout and handle. The wooden knob surmounting the lid is an unusual feature.

SILVER COFFEE AND TEA SERVICE, 1912 (above)

American architect George Washington Maher designed this richly ornamented service for Rockledge, the Minnesota home he designed for E. G. King. Consistent with the Arts and Crafts ethos, Maher's designs for its furniture, table-ware, lighting fixtures, and other accoutrements echoed the Palladian motif of the long, low stucco house with its segmented arches. Early in his career, Maher worked as an apprentice draftsman alongside Frank Lloyd Wright.

JOSEF HOFFMANN SILVER COFFEE SERVICE *(above)*

Austrian Josef Hoffmann, architect, designer, and cofounder of Vienna's Wiener Werkstätte, was known for his elegant symmetrical designs for metalware. From 1903 most of them were executed by the Wiener Werkstätte, whose principles owed much to the influence of C. R. Mackintosh of the Glasgow School and Secessionist Otto Wagner, with whom Hoffmann had studied and collaborated. With financial backing from textile heir Fritz Warndorfer, and many private commissions, the Werkstätte spared no expense for materials, accepting elitism as a concomitant of its mission of design reform.

C. R. MACKINTOSH CUTLERY (right)

The severe geometry of this fish knife and fork set is typical of Mackintosh's modernism, which combined predominantly straight lines with gentle curves. First and foremost an architect, his primary concern in all his decorative work was to complement the buildings and interiors he designed, from Glasgow's Hill House to the city's revolutionary School of Arts (1897).

C. R. ASHBEE CUTLERY, 1900–02 (below)

Made by Ashbee's own Guild of Handicraft, these pieces reflect the influence of William Morris in their sensitivity to natural forms. They were executed during the period when Ashbee moved his School and Guild from London's East End to the Cotswolds. A Romantic socialist at heart, Ashbee made a significant break with Victorian tradition and was the principal organizer of the British Arts and Crafts Movement. He had a notable influence on American architect Frank Lloyd Wright and lectured frequently in Chicago from 1900. In 1909 he published Modern English Silverwork.

PERIOD CHANDELIER (above)

This chandelier was probably produced c. 1900 by Philip J. Handel, whose Handel Company was established in Meriden, Connecticut, in 1885 to produce decorative lamps and lighting fixtures. From 1900 there was a branch factory in New York City. Handel's products resembled those of Louis C. Tiffany, but were less expensive. The company's later designs tended toward the Art Nouveau style.

GUSTAV STICKLEY COPPER CHANDELIER (right)

The Craftsman Studios produced this hand wrought five-light chandelier (Style No. 401) with bell-shaped amber glass shades. Embossed or cut-out hearts were often used to ornament Stickley's popular lighting fixtures.

ELIZABETH EATON BURTON LAMP, C. 1905 (right)

Santa Barbara, California, artist Elizabeth Eaton Burton combined hammered copper, copper tubing, and abalone shells to produce an iridescent effect in her electrical lamps, which are her best-known metalworks. Born in Paris, she emigrated to California to work with her father, landscaper Charles Frederic Eaton, in the flourishing Santa Barbara Arts and Crafts community.

HEINTZ ART METAL LAMP (left)

Brothers Otto L. and Edwin A. Heintz began their careers as metalworkers at Buffalo, New York's, Art Craft Shop around 1900. Within six years, they had established their reputation for handcrafted copper and bronze lamps, vases, desk sets, and other accessories, as well as gold and silver jewelry, which they produced under the auspices of Heintz Art Metal until about 1930.

DIRK VAN ERP LAMP, C. 1910 *(above)*

This handwrought copper lamp, with its flaring base and conical mica shade, is typical of the work done by Dutch-born metalsmith van Erp after he emigrated to Oakland, California, where he set up a workshop in 1908. Two years later he moved to San Francisco, where the Dirk van Erp

Studio produced a wealth of sought-after art metal objects until long after his retirement in 1929. The studio was best known for its electrical lamps, with mica shades shellacked to produce an amber light, and for imposing copper pottery patined deep red.

ROYCROFT BEATEN COPPER LAMP, C. 1910 (right)

Roycroft was one of the few commercially successful and long-lasting Arts and Crafts communities, largely because its founder, Elbert Hubbard, was an experienced businessman who pioneered mass-marketing techniques. At its height, Roycroft employed more than 400 craftsmen in working conditions that were ideal by early 20th-century standards: 8-hour workdays, good housing, libraries, training programs, and other amenities. C. R. Ashbee's wife Janet compared Hubbard to "Ruskin and Morris with a good strong American flavour."

PERIOD LAMP WITH TRANSLUCENT BANDED SHADE (left)

One of the most attractive features of many Arts and Crafts lighting fixtures was the subdued "natural" light filtered through shades of mica (also called isinglass) and other translucent materials, including silk gauze and a variety of shells: abalone, chiton, limpet, pearl, and Philippine of varying colors. Elegant art-metalwork base, banding, and finial enhance the beauty of this decorative lamp.

ARCHIBALD KNOX SILVER BOX WITH GEMSTONES (below)

The interlacing Celtic-style design on this ornamental box resembles that on the Knox tea service on page 114 (top). The decorative motifs of Celtic art were widely employed by period metalsmiths, especially those of the Glasgow school, and gave a look of hand craftsmanship even to machine-made pieces. The use of unfaceted semiprecious gemstones, highly polished, also harks back to the incomparable metal-work of 7th-century Hiberno-Saxon artists, who worked out their complex patterns in garnets and colored glass.

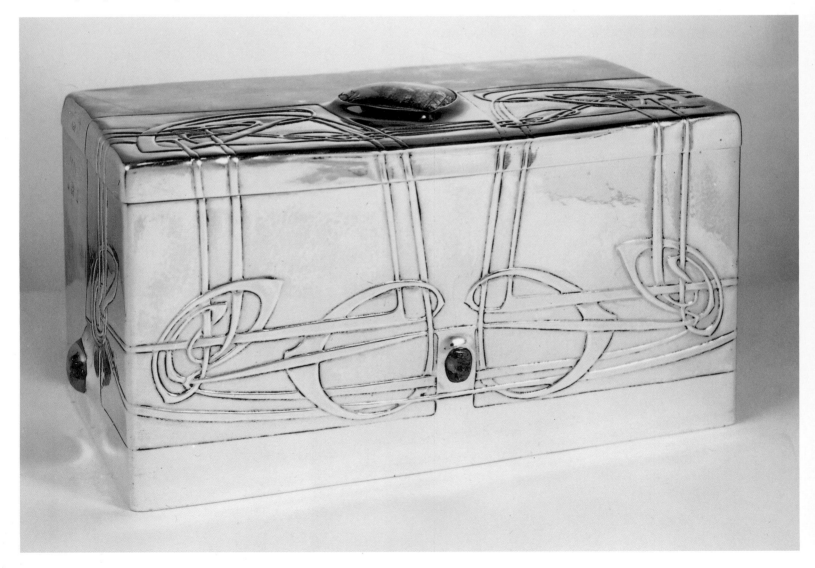

ELVERHOJ COLONY NECKLACE, C. 1913–20 *(left)*

Crafted of gold, pearl, and tourmaline, this 14-inch necklace is typical of the jewelry made by the Elverhoj Colony near Poughkeepsie, New York. Founded in 1913 by Johannes Morton and A. H. Anderson, the community offered courses in printing, etching, jewelry, weaving, metalwork, and bookbinding. It was best known for its gold and silver jewelry, which incorporated semiprecious stones and shells into designs drawn from local flowers.

JAHN BROOCH IN THE FORM OF AN ANGEL *(right)*

The Pre-Raphaelite influence is apparent in this brooch from the collection of the Victoria and Albert Museum, in which the angel has the face of a young man. The simplicity, purity, and idealism of Early Renaissance art was a source of inspiration for many Arts and Crafts designers.

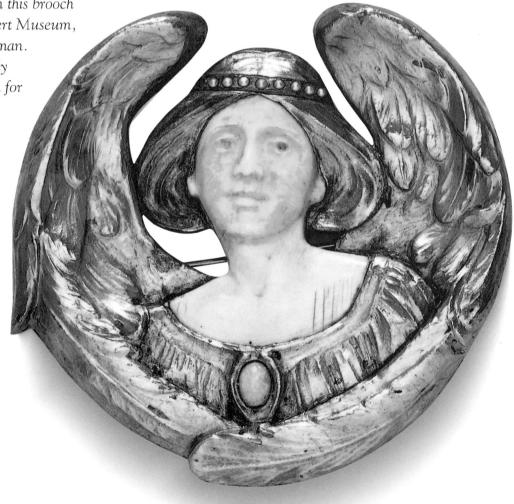

⊞ TEXTILES

The impetus for Morris's early experiments in the field of textiles was the construction of the Red House. "Nothing can be a work of art which is not useful," declared Morris, as he invited friends Burne-Jones, Rossetti, Webb, and others to help create furnishings for his new home. Morris's major contribution was in textiles, including an embroidered hanging bearing his motto "If I Can." Indeed he could, and did, revive this ancient craft: embroidered wall hangings would become a feature of every Morris interior. Some of the earliest designs were inspired by medieval manuscripts. For the dining room of the Red House, Morris planned twelve large embroidered panels depicting characters from Chaucer's *Legende of Good Women* (seven of these were com-

pleted). While Morris researched traditional stitches and created the designs, his wife (who served as the model for the figure in the St. Catherine panel) undertook the actual sewing.

In 1871 Morris discovered and rented Kelmscott Manor, some 20 miles west of Oxford, where he continued his experiments in sewing, weaving, and textile design, and in 1878 he established carpet looms in the stable blocks at the rear of Kelmscott House in Hammersmith, London. Morris's interest in textiles was fostered by his experience in assisting Henry Cole in the collection of carpets, embroideries and tapestries, particularly those of Middle-Eastern origin, for the South Kensington Museum. Morris's own Hammersmith rugs, which were hand knotted, sometimes carry the trademark of a letter M and a hammer over a symbol of the River Thames.

In May 1878, Morris set up a high-ware loom in his bedroom at Kelmscott House and taught himself tapestry making. The Cabbage and Vine tapestry was completed in September after 516 working hours. In 1881 the main Morris and Company operations moved from Hammersmith to Merton Abbey in Surrey, where there was more space for looms and a plentiful supply of the clean water required for textile dyeing (the Thames had grown increasingly polluted). As an alternative to the acid colors of the new chemical dyes, Morris turned his attention to creating permanent vegetable dyes and to the indigo discharge technique for dyeing chintzes. In this process, the cloth is first dyed all over in an indigo vat; the pattern is then printed with a bleaching reagent which reduces or removes the blue as the pattern

Below: Hand-printing chintz at Morris and Company's Merton Abbey Workshops, set up in 1881 to produce the textiles that made Morris's name a byword for elegant fabrics for the Arts and Crafts interior.

requires. The process continued through mordants and madder vats, welds and boiling soaps to produce a quality of color unmatched by many industrial dyes even after a hundred years.

While Morris and his contemporaries achieved commercial success with their sophisticated (and costly) designs and products, the impetus for the revival of hand weaving was provided by Ruskin. During the 1870s, he took up the cause of the hand-spinners on the Isle of Man, acquired a water mill for them, and encouraged them to produce high-quality woolen cloth. Toward the end of his life, Ruskin also did much to revive cottage textile industries in Westmoreland and Cumbria: the Langdale Weaving Industry set up by Albert Fleming in 1883 and Annie Garnett's Windermere Spinnery (from 1891) were established with Ruskin's encouragement. Other workshops followed in Haslemere (Peasant Industries) in the 1890s. The London School of Weaving was founded by Katie Graset in 1898, while the Home Arts and Industries Association, established in 1884, dedicated itself to teaching a wide range of hand skills like spinning, knitting, tailoring, and sewing.

In Europe, the *Handarbetets Vannar* (Friends of Textile Art Association) was established in Sweden as early as 1814 with the aim of reviving traditional techniques and styles. Many Scandinavian associations focused on textiles — considered a "pure" peasant art — while others, like the *Foreningen Svensk Hemslojd* (Swedish Handicraft Society), founded in 1899, studied and collected all country crafts. Both types of groups not only preserved and copied the old, but used traditional models as the basis for new work.

In Finland, Gallen-Kallela (1865–1931) modernized the traditional Finnish knotting technique called the *ryijy* by applying it to strong geometric patterns, while in Norway Gerhard Munthe (1849–1929) pioneered a revival of tapestry weaving with traditional techniques and subjects taken from folk tales but rendered in a modern style. Frida Hansen (1855–1931) also used tales from the Norwegian sagas but invented a new method of tapestry weaving whereby parts of the warp were left exposed.

Above: *Gerhard Munthe tapestry, c. 1900, woven in Norway by* Den Norst Husflod. *Entitled* "Villarkonn" (*Forgetful Potion*), *it depicts the folksong heroine Little Kirsten receiving a magic potion brewed by the trolls so that she will forget the human world and remain with them.*

Above: *American period textiles hand-embroidered in silk. Many manufacturers, including Gustav Stickley and H. E. Varren Company, marketed needlework kits and materials for embroidery, crewel work, fringing, and knitting. Decorative silk thread was made by firms like the Cheney Brothers of Connecticut, who also produced designs by Candace Wheeler and Associated Artists.*

In Hungary, crafts and buildings of Transylvania (now part of Romania) were considered the oldest, and home industry associations were founded there. The region later became the center for the study of vernacular design. The *Gödöllō* artists colony executed designs for tapestries using traditional techniques like the *Kalim* and *Torontal* (from the south and the east of Hungary) with pure vegetable dyes. Peasant craftsmen and -women of Kalotaszeg were encouraged to continue producing the stylized floral embroidery of their traditional dress.

A similar historical revivalism was taking place in the United States, manifested on the one hand in the romanticized image of Native American tribes living in close harmony with nature, and on the other, in the reinterpretation of American Colonial style. Navajo blankets—used as rugs by Arts and Crafts collectors—were prized for their origin on handmade looms from designs dating to pre-Columbian days and preserved through myths and legends. (Increased demand for such blankets in the late nineteenth century resulted in a decline in quality until the Native American renaissance of

the early twentieth century, still ongoing.)

When hand weaving was revived and became popular, rag rugs were among the articles produced by American Arts and Crafts weavers. Traditionally, as the name suggests, worn-out material was used as weft, but over time, the warp became commercially produced cotton. Weavers began cutting up new material for the weft in order to control color placements and patterns. Rag-rug weaving was undertaken by the Hingham (Massachusetts) Society of Arts and Crafts, primarily for use in bedrooms and bathrooms. Usually, the rugs were some five feet long and three feet wide (the standard loom width) and were used as occasional rugs. However, examples survive of room-sized rugs of up to three separate loom widths sewn together.

In New York, Candace Wheeler's needlework and embroidery led the revival in fine textile crafts. Her success in using her artistry professionally, rather than as a hobby, was widely emulated by members of the Society for Decorative Arts and affluent women who saw their work. The primary textile group in Massachusetts was the Society of Blue and White Needlework, founded in Deerfield in 1896 by Ellen Millet and Mary Whiting to preserve the decorative art of 18-century needlewomen. Most of the society's early work was done in blue and white linen yarns on linen or cotton foundation cloths; later, more colors were added, including green, pink, and brown yarns and fabrics dyed with various natural substances like indigo, madder, and butternut, as in Colonial times. The society focused its efforts on teaching local women embroidery skills rather than on selling its products. Eventually, its work was widely exhibited, winning prizes at the 1901 Pan-American Exposition and the Panama-Pacific Exposition of 1915. It was the success of the Society of Blue and White Needlework that fostered establishment of the Deerfield Society of Arts and Crafts, whose members made rugs, baskets, furniture, and jewelry.

One phenomenon of the Arts and Crafts movement in the United States was the establishment of schools for needlework and other crafts. Sybil Carter, a missionary with the Episcopal Church, introduced lacemaking classes on Indian reservations to provide manual training in a new skill congenial to Native American artisans, who excelled in bead and quillwork, weaving, and basketmaking, depending upon their tribal heritage. At Berea college, in rural Kentucky, William Frost encouraged local families to weave "Kivers" or bed coverlets to earn money for education. Another craftsman who helped spread basic weaving skills to a wider American audience was Edward Wurst (1866–1949), the author of several books including *Foot-Power Loom Weaving* (1918), still considered a classic manual for hand loom weavers. In New York City, the *Scuola d'Industrie Italiene*, (School of Italian Work) was set up to improve the conditions of Italian immigrant women and their daughters and to encourage the manufacture of traditional laces and embroideries.

Natural textiles and colors were popular not only for Arts and Crafts home furnishings, but for the "Reform" styles in women's clothing that put new emphasis on comfort, quality, and utility. May Morris, the daughter and disciple of William Morris, helped spread the gospel of fashion reform, and women were encouraged to favor simple, practical, printed cotton over elegant silk, lace, and whalebone corsets. Washability became more important with the decline of domestic service, as more women undertook their own housework: cotton and linen lawn and tub-silk (a cotton and silk blend) became popular, as did sturdy linen lace, crochet, and coarse-thread embroidered napery and accessories. The Arts and Crafts-minded homemaker took both her domestic and aesthetic responsibilities seriously.

Below: Catherine Tobin Wright, Frank Lloyd Wright's first wife, wears an informal dress of the type espoused by May Morris, William Morris's younger daughter, and others in the movement to reform women's clothing in favor of comfort and ease of care. The Wrights' Oak Park, Illinois, home/studio was a laboratory for movement ideas and innovations.

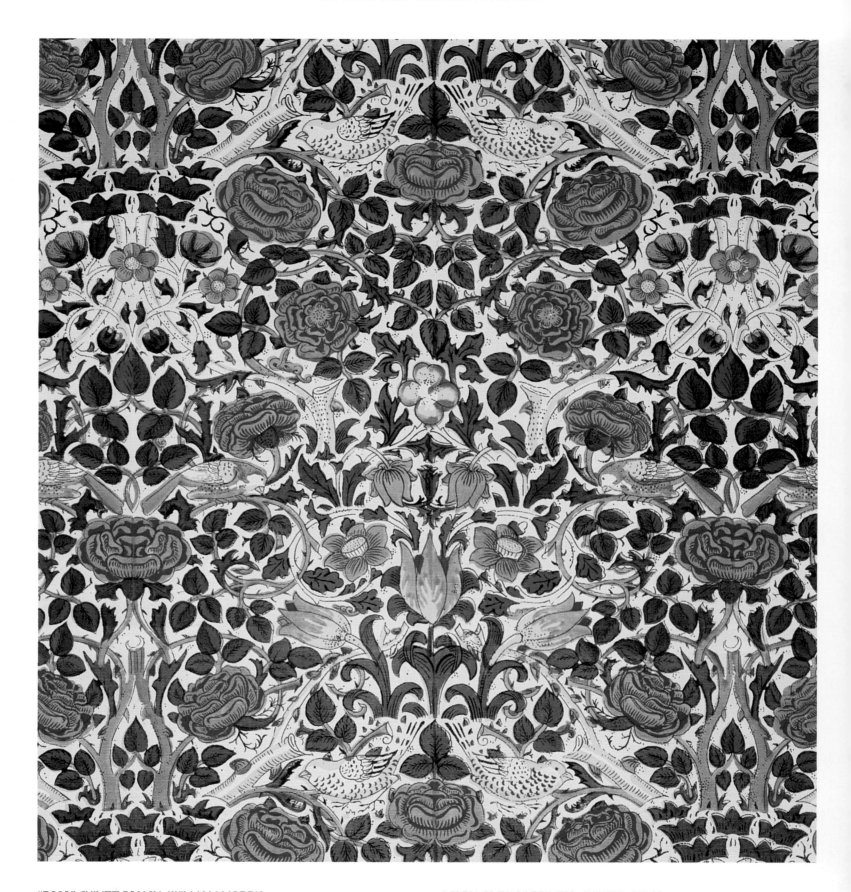

"ROSE" CHINTZ DESIGN, WILLIAM MORRIS *(above)*
A rich and exuberant design produced by William Morris's Merton Abbey workshop, this decorative textile features roses, tulips, and other popular cottage-garden flowers, with stylized birds, in vivid shades of pink, red, gold, orange, and green.

"CORN COCKLE" PRINTED CHINTZ, C.1883 *(opposite)*
This Morris design from the Merton Abbey workshop was inspired by a common English field and roadside flower, in keeping with the Arts and Crafts aesthetic that found new beauty in native plants and materials.

"ROSE TREE" PANEL, NEW ENGLAND (above)

This embroidered hanging from c. 1905, by an anonymous craftswoman, features a rose tree appliquéd on a coarse linen background in smoother madder-dyed linen. The foreground carries appliquéd irises in violet linen and scattered small flowers; the horizon is softened with rows of darning stitch.

"WOODPECKER" TAPESTRY, WILLIAM MORRIS, C. 1881 (above)

The "Woodpecker" tapestry was designed by William Morris and woven at Morris & Company, Merton Abbey, in 1881. The popularity of Morris's incomparable textile, wallpaper, and tapestry designs has endured down to the present.

"CROMER BIRD," A. H. MACKMURDO. *(above)*
*This design on printed cotton cretonne was produced by
the Century Guild after 1882 and embodies Mackmurdo's
characteristic lightness and flow of rhythmic forms.*

"FLYING FISH," DEERFIELD, MASSACHUSETTS *(above)*
Embroidered on linen, this design from the early 1900s comprises a line of three fish worked in linen rope thread and two layers of satin stitch for a three-dimensional effect. The series of waves, worked in outline and chain stitch, has subtle gradations of color.

"POLLY'S PARROT" BUREAU COVER, DEERFIELD *(right)*
This engaging design was adapted from an 18th-century embroidery by Polly Wright (1752–1821) of Deerfield by the Deerfield Society of Blue and White Needlework, formed to preserve the artistry of Colonial needlewomen. The material is linen on linen, 14¾ x 43½".

AMERICAN "DRAGONFLY" EMBROIDERY, INDIGO GROUND *(right)*

*Diligent American craftswomen experimented with many
vegetable dyes originally used by Colonial artisans, some of
them adopted, in turn, from Native American dyemakers.
Fabrics and threads were colored with indigo, madder, and
fustic, with gray and brown shades derived from such trees
as butternut, walnut, maple, and sumac.*

DEERFIELD BLUE AND WHITE SOCIETY DOILY *(below)*

*This impeccably worked nine-inch doily has no fewer than
six kinds of stitchery: outline, New England laid, feather,
satin, herringbone, and cross-stitch so fine that it could be
identified only with a magnifying glass. The borders of round
doilies were always worked in close New England laid stitch
and trimmed so carefully that the embroidery threads were
never cut.*

BATTYE EMBROIDERED PANEL, MAY MORRIS *(above)*

This detailed design by May Morris, with its heraldic and chivalric themes, shows the artistry of a gifted designer in the vanguard of the Arts and Crafts Movement. Morris lived and worked in Hammersmith, western London, and traveled widely to lecture on her father's work and the design ethos of the movement.

NORWEGIAN PICTURE TAPESTRY *(opposite)*

Woven in Gudbransdal from a late 17th-/early 18th-century design, this linen and wool billedvev (picture tapestry) depicts the Adoration of the Magi. Balthasar is at bottom right, Melchior at bottom left, and Caspar at top left. At top right, the magi kneel before the Virgin Mary and the Christ Child. Note that most of the letters of the inscription were woven backward and some upside down. The inscription translates "The Great Holy Three Kings Coming from Sheba."

GRAPHIC ARTS

allpaper designs by Morris and other British designers, together with sketches and studies for textile and stained glass designs, were the earliest expressions of the Arts and Crafts Movement in the graphic arts. Motifs from nature were the dominant themes, while the stylistic influences of Japanese, Romantic, and Pre-Raphaelite art are evident.

The private press movement owed much to the inspiration provided by Arthur Heygate Mackmurdo's journal *Hobby Horse*. The first issue, edited jointly by Mackmurdo and Herbert Horne, was published in April 1884 with a line-block cover designed by Selwyn Image, cofounder with Mackmurdo of the Century Guild. There was a two-year hiatus before the second issue appeared in 1886.

One of the first art-oriented literary magazines of the 1880s, the *Hobby Horse* had a number of distinguished contributors, including Ruskin, Ford Madox Brown, Rossetti, G.F Watts, Burne-Jones, W.B Yeats, and Oscar Wilde. It was the first magazine to treat graphics as an art form, and it introduced contemporary British design and design theory to the Continent. Belgian architect Henri Van der Velde subscribed to *Hobby Horse*, and Victor Horta reportedly used a Century Guild wallpaper in his Tassel House. Its most important effect, however, was the part it played in encouraging William Morris to establish his Kelmscott Press.

Morris's last venture in the pursuit of good design was to revive the art of the printed book, to which end he founded the Kelmscott Press near his Hammersmith home, Kelmscott House. When Morris died six years later, he had issued over fifty titles, including *Chaucer*, *The Nature of Gothic*, and his own *Earthly Paradise*. His monochrome art books, many of them printed to designs by Edward Burne-Jones, were produced in limited editions for a select market. They addressed the declining standards inherent in the introduction of machine techniques in printing for a mass market.

Morris conceived a book in architectural terms: each detail contributed to the whole, so all the elements—paper, inks,

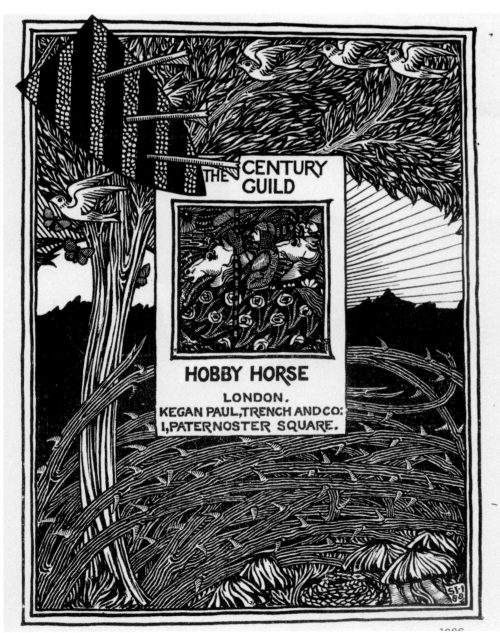

Below: *Front cover of the Century Guild's* Hobby Horse *magazine (1886), designed by Selwyn Image and published in London by Kegan Paul, Trench and Company (now Routledge & Kegan Paul).*

typeforms, spacing between the words and lines, integration of text, illustrations, and decorations—related to the overall design. This concern led Morris to have his paper handmade in Kent and to import his inks from Hanover. His dissatisfaction with commercially available typefaces resulted in his own designs including Golden, Troy, and Chaucer.

The first Kelmscott Press book, Morris's *Story of the Glittering Plain*, appeared in 1891. Printed from the Golden font, its two-page spreads were treated as a single unit rather than as two distinct pages, with closely spaced lines and headings set in upper-case letters flush left rather than centered on the page. The result was a handmade, limited-edition work of art with decorations that recall the incunabula of fifteenth-century Europe.

One of the first Americans to show the influence of Morris's book design in his work was Daniel Berkeley Updike (1860–1944) who established his own Merrymount Press in 1893. At first, it was closely aligned with the avant-garde group in Boston that published the Elziver Press magazines *Knight Errant* and *Mahogany Tree*. In 1896, the year the Kelmscott Press issued *Chaucer*, Updike brought out the masterwork of American Arts and Crafts printing, *The Altar Book.* The wood block engravings were the work of British artist Robert Anning Bell, and the overall design was that of architect Bertram Grosvenor Goodhue (1869–1924) who also designed the largest reredos in any Gothic church for St. Thomas's in New York City. For *The Altar Book*, Goodhue created the borders, initials, binding, and typeface, called, appropriately, Merrymount. The demands of his architectural practice eventually forced Goodhue to abandon book design, but not before he had created

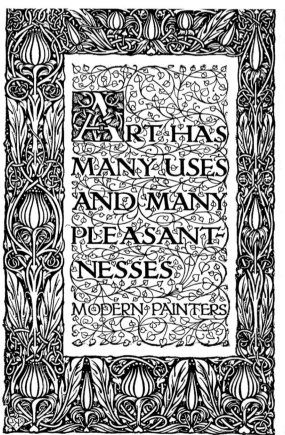
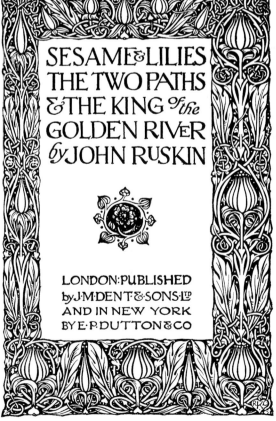

Left: *Title page for a compendium of Ruskin lectures and the fairy tale* The King of the Golden River, *an allegory on human stewardship of the earth. Both Gothic and Oriental influences are clearly seen in the decorative borders, initials, and typography.*

GRAPHIC ARTS

Below: *Shakespearean actress Ellen Terry as Ophelia, in a book illustration by E. Gordon Craig.*

title pages, decorations, initials, and type-faces for all the major presses that made Boston a center for the revival of fine-art printing: Copeland & Day, Stone & Kimball, and Small & Maynard.

The international revolution in book production and typography in the 1890s brought other private presses into being,

including C.R. Ashbee's Essex House Press; the Ashendene Press, founded by St. John Hornby in 1894; Charles Rickett's Vale Press; Lucien Pissarro's Eragny Press; and the Doves Press, founded by T.J. Cobden-Sanderson and Emery Walker in 1900. All had received their initial impetus from William Morris, but their achievements and styles were varied and individualistic.

During the 1890s, book and periodical publishers began to use posters to advertise new titles. Manufacturers also turned to this attractive medium and commissioned posters that were often issued in limited editions like fine prints. Magazines appeared devoted entirely to this subject. Will Bradley (1868–1962), in his poster for *Bradley: His Book* (1896), reflected the new popularity of posters and little magazines, as they were called. Bradley became known for the posters he designed for Stone & Kimball's *The Chap-Book*, the periodical that launched the

American little-magazine movement in 1894. *The Chap-Book*, which appeared from 1894 to 1898, combined avant-garde content with a format like that of the pamphlets sold by itinerant peddlers into the seventeenth century. Bradley's own publication, *Bradley: His Book*, of which seven issues were printed in 1896–7, used color and typography in ways befitting Bradley's status in American typography. After 1900 he undertook less bookwork, but his commercial work gained even greater influence with the appearance of the *American Chap-Book*, (1904–05), a periodical commissioned by American Type Founders Company to advertise its wares to American printers. By this time, Bradley's style had moved away from the Morris influence and evolved into a personal version of Arts and Crafts graphics.

One of the most important journals to spread the aesthetic principles and philosophy of the Arts and Crafts Movement was the British magazine *The Studio*, launched in 1893 by the Arts and Crafts Exhibition Society. From the first issue, which helped to make the reputation of Aubrey Beardsley, *The Studio* was concerned with new trends in art and design. This made it the ideal vehicle for disseminating both Arts and Crafts ideologies and the emergent Art Nouveau style. *The Studio* enjoyed rapid international success: in Barcelona, it was read by the young Picasso, and in St. Petersburg, by ballet impresario Sergei Diaghilev. Numerous European and American journals were founded on this model, including the Austrian *Ver Scarum* and the German *Pan* and *Dekorative Kunst*.

In the United States, Gustav Stickley's widely read journal *The Craftsman* and *Handicraft*, published by the Boston Society of Arts and Crafts, influenced architects, interior designers, and ordinary people alike. The *Ladies' Home Journal* published Frank Lloyd Wright's Prairie House designs in the early 1900s, and *House and Garden* and *The House Beautiful* did their part to promote integration of life and art in the everyday environment.

The Arts and Crafts Exhibition Society's first show in Brussels helped to inspire the Belgian group *L'Association Pour L'Art*,. Still more significant was its impact on *Les Vignt*. Belgium became especially prominent in the graphic arts. *Les Vignt's* 1891 catalogue carried a design by George Lemman that recalls the curling lines of Gauguin's paintings. The following year, Henri Van der Velde turned to book design and produced the title page for Max Elskamp's *Dominical*; here, too, the serpentine lines of waves breaking on the beach are reminiscent of Gauguin's treatment of water in his painting *Man with an Axe* (1891). The typographic revival begun by Mackmurdo and Morris was carried on in Germany by Otto Eckmann, who designed an alphabet and cover for Ruskin's *Seven Lamps of Architecture* in 1900, and by Peter Behrens (1868–1940) who designed typefaces in the Art Nouveau style.

Opposite, right: Fine Art Society poster for an exhibition of designs by Walter Crane, an influential member of the Art Workers' Guild.

Above: Ornamental headings for pictorial essays on American country homes and gardens, published by The Ladies Home Journal in March 1899. The Philadelphia-based magazine published Arts and Crafts designs and adopted styles typical of the movement in its graphic design. In these panels, subject and design merge into a unified expression. The crosshatching and brickwork on the walls provide a geometric counterpoint to the rounded, organic forms.

"DAISY" WALLPAPER DESIGN, WILLIAM MORRIS *(above)*
A richly textured design in shades of pink, red, white, gold, and sage green, this wallpaper was first produced c. 1864 by the firm of Morris, Marshall, Faulkner & Company. Based in London's Red Lion Square, the firm was a collaborative venture in the decorative arts in which Morris's friends and artist members executed much of the work.

"ROSE & BUTTERFLY" WALLPAPER, CENTURY GUILD *(above)*
This elegant pastel pattern was designed by A. H. Mackmurdo, who founded the Century Guild in 1882 with the primary objective of reforming British design. As a youth, he traveled in Italy and France with Ruskin, a family friend, to study nature and architecture in light of the unity underlying all organic form. The Century Guild produced some of Great Britain's most important 19th-century work.

"FRUIT" WALLPAPER DESIGN, WILLIAM MORRIS *(opposite)*
This early design signaled a shift from the ornate Victorian style of the mid-1800s to a freer, flowing mode that celebrated nature as seen by the discerning eye of the artist.

When Adam delved and Eve span
Who was then the gentleman

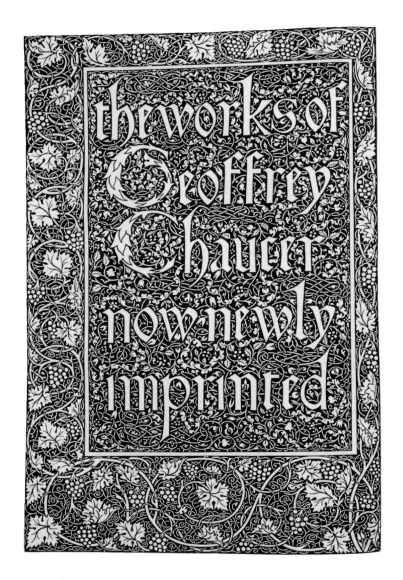

FRONTISPIECE, MORRIS ROMANCE, 1888 *(opposite)*

A drawing by Edward Burne-Jones, with lettering by William Morris, for his book A Dream of John Ball. The Romantic influence is seen in the idealized figures of Adam and Eve at work digging and spinning, with cherubic children at Eve's feet. Morris's publications were monochrome artworks, designed to be the antithesis of the crude commercial printing of the day. Many private presses sprang up to emulate his efforts, in Great Britain and abroad.

KELMSCOTT PRESS EDITION OF CHAUCER, 1869 *(above)*

Morris undertook to revive the art of the printed book when he set up the Kelmscott Press in Hammersmith, London. This title page and first page of his Chaucer form a single design unit, from the curling grapevine borders to the ruled illustrations and ornate capitals in the Medieval style. The typeface, Chaucer, was also designed by Morris.

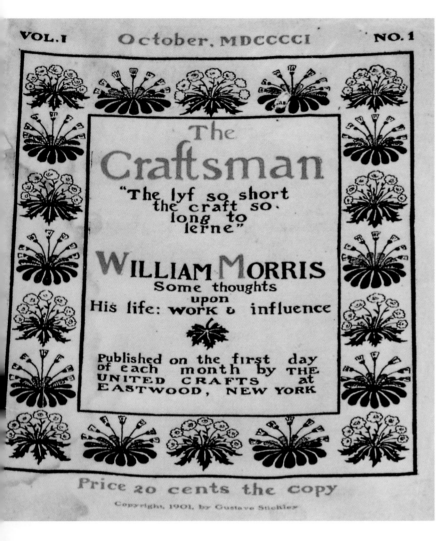

FIRST EDITION, "CRAFTSMAN" MAGAZINE, 1901 (above)

Gustav Stickley's magazine The Craftsman was the single greatest disseminator of Arts and Crafts ideals in America. Published monthly at Syracuse, New York, by Stickley's Craftsman workshops, it aimed to make good design available to the growing middle class. Stickley's design for furniture and moderately priced Craftsman Homes influenced other publications and made his magazine a forum for urban and suburban planning.

"CRAFTSMAN" COVER FROM 1904 (above, right)

While Stickley continued to promote such Morrisian ideals as education, labor, and social reform, The Craftsman became increasingly pragmatic as Stickley's enterprises flourished throughout the early 1900s. The magazine advertised and showcased many of this firm's products, but respect for sound design and honest workmanship remained dominant until the magazine ceased publishing in 1916.

NEWCOMB COLLEGE YEARBOOK, 1903 (opposite, above)

The illustration shows students at work in the pottery that made the small New Orleans women's college nationally known for its ceramic art wares. The whimsical borders at top and bottom left show the Arts and Crafts influence on American graphic design, which tended toward simplicity and everyday themes.

JAMES WHITCOMB RILEY CALENDAR BOOK, 1912 (opposite)

This book by American poet James Whitcomb Riley had 12 woodcut illustrations in color by artist Gustave Baumann. "November" is a detailed depiction of a rural household settling in for the long winter months. Riley's folksy poems made him one of America's best-loved writers.

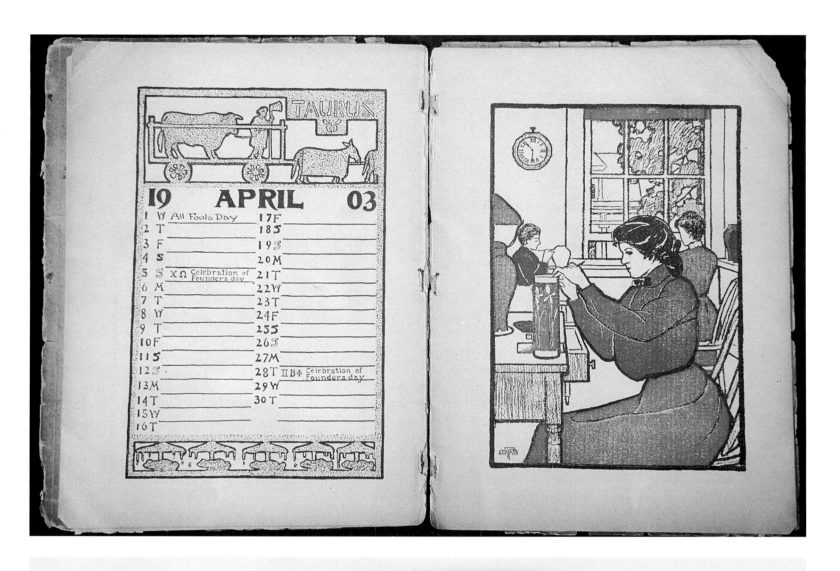

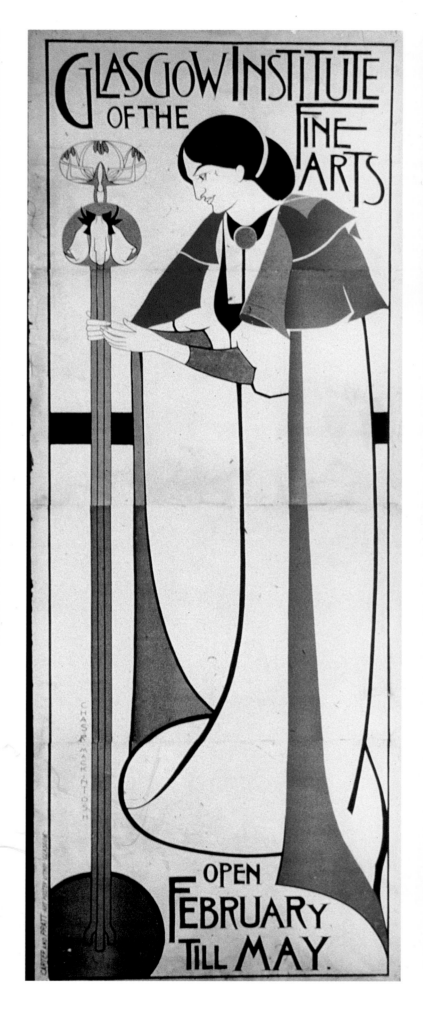

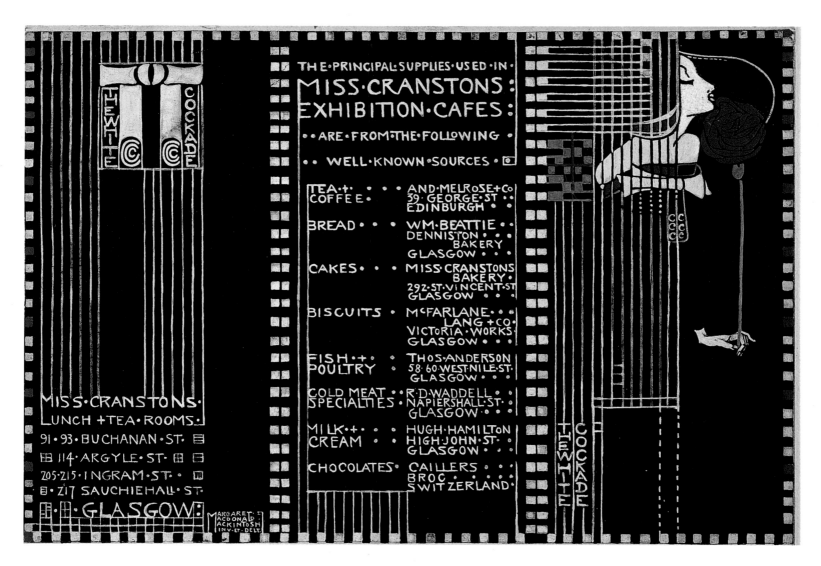

C. R. MACKINTOSH POSTER, PERIODICAL *(far left)*

Executed in 1896, this is one of three poster designs by C. R. Mackintosh. The Scottish Musical Review was a short-lived periodical published in Glasgow from 1894 to 1897. The rigidly symmetrical design incorporates stylized songbirds and an unconventional abstraction of the human form that provoked ridicule at the time. The muted color lithography, in shades of blue, green, purple, and brown, is evocative of the Scottish landscape.

MACKINTOSH POSTER, GLASGOW INSTITUTE *left)*

This more conventional design from c. 1894–6 is for the Glasgow Institute of the Fine Arts. It reflects the economy of Japanese art and the elongated austerity that earned Mackintosh and his three principal collaborators the nickname of the "Spook School." From the 1890s, Mackintosh worked both independently and together with Herbert MacNair and the sisters Frances and Margaret Macdonald. Margaret married Mackintosh in 1900.

MARGARET MACDONALD MACKINTOSH MENU DESIGN *(above)*

This design for the White Cockade Cafe shows the artistry of Margaret Macdonald Mackintosh, one of the Glasgow designers sometimes called "the Four." She collaborated with C. R. Mackintosh on several interiors, including that of Hill House; designed furniture and wall panels in repoussé metal and painted gesso; and produced textile designs as well as print graphics.

WILL BRADLEY POSTER, EARLY 1900S (above)
American graphic artist Will Bradley had a taut, linear style and a tendency to fill the entire page space, as seen in this striking poster design.

BRADLEY WOODCUT POSTER, 1896 (opposite)
Designed to advertise Bradley's art magazine, published 1896–7, this poster illustrates his innovative use of line and color. Bradley was influential in many spheres, including architecture, furniture, and fittings.

ACKNOWLEDGEMENTS

The publisher would like to thank the following people for their assistance in preparing this book: Elizabeth Montgomery, for picture research assistance and the loan of antiquarian books and prints; Claire Gordon, for preparing the index; Jill Thomas-Clark for advice on the glass section; Emily Head; Kate Hunt; and the following agencies and individuals who provided illustrations:

Corning Museum of Glass: 2 (left), 54, 55, 56, 57 (left), 58 (both), 61, 62, 63, 65, 66, 67.

©**Eva Heyd**: 109, 113 (right), 117 (top).

Hunterian Art Gallery, University of Glasgow, Mackintosh Collection: 32 (both), 33, 64, 111 (top), 140 (both), 141.

©**A. F. Kersting**: 8, 9, 28, 29 (both).

© **Balthazar Korab**: 18, 34, 35, 40, 41 (right), 42, 43, 44 (both), 45 (both), 46, 47 (both).

Lee M. Friedman Fund, courtesy, Museum of Fine Arts, Boston: 142.

©**Elizabeth Montgomery**: 26.

Pocumtuck Valley Memorial Association, Memorial Hall Museum, Deerfield, Massachusetts: 124 (left), 126 (both), 127 (both).

©**David Rago**: 2 (right), 12, 13, 15 (both), 16, 17, 19, 22, 23, 24, 36 (both), 37 (both), 38 (both), 39, 48, 52, 59 (both), 72, 73, 74 (both), 75, 80, 88, 89 (all), 90, 91 (both), 92 (both), 93 (all), 94 (both), 95 (both), 96 (both), 97 (both), 100, 102 (both), 103 (both), 104, 105 (both), 108 (bottom), 110, 112 (both), 113 (left), 114, 115 (both), 120, 138 (both), 139 (both).

Courtesy of St. Paul's Episcopal Church, Stockbridge, Massachusetts: 51.

Vesterheim Norwegian-American Museum: 119, 129.

Courtesy of the Trustees of the Victoria and Albert Museum: 41 (left), 53, 57 (right), 60 (photo, Daniel McGrath), 70, 71, 77 (both), 78, 79, 81, 82, 83, 84, 85, 86, 87, 98, 99, 107, 108 (top), 111 (bottom), 116, 117 (bottom).

The William Morris Gallery, Walthamstow, London: 3, 7, 10, 30 (both), 31, 49, 68, 76, 106, 118, 122, 123, 124 (right), 125, 128, 130, 134, 135 (both), 136, 137.

Frank Lloyd Wright Home and Studio Foundation: 14, 121, 14 (negative H&S H 273), 121 (negative H&S H 180).

⠿ INDEX